ADVANCE PRAISE FOR
ENTREPRENEURIAL LIFE

"I have often found that people who are described as financial entrepreneurs normally showed at a young age that they wanted to earn a profit, quickly understood that they had to render a worthwhile service, and as they matured realized that they were limited only by their abilities and desire to continue to grow. Since the day I met Bob Luddy working out of a truck he has shown all the qualities the great leaders possess, and I know his personal growth will continue. It has been a pleasure to watch his company grow."

JAMES H. MAYNARD
CO-FOUNDER AND CHAIRMAN, GOLDEN CORRAL

"When someone 'succeeds' it is legitimate to ask oneself what is the key of his success. Several replies are possible: and there is one which in the case of Bob Luddy is appropriate. Talent, hard work, courage, perseverance, learning the art of defeating defeats: these attributes describe Bob. But there is still one factor often forgotten: the beautiful virtue of gratitude; because success in the most beautiful sense of this word, is never achieved without the help of others."

DR. ALICE VON HILDEBRAND
RETIRED PROFESSOR OF PHILOSOPHY, HUNTER COLLEGE

"This book has the rare quality of being able to combine practical, real-life experience, economic erudition and moral sensitivity all in one package. It is a true gem and worthy of a wide readership."

REV. ROBERT A. SIRICO
PRESIDENT AND CO-FOUNDER, ACTON INSTITUTE

"Mr. Luddy is an unapologetic capitalist, a man of deep principle whose second-greatest satisfaction in his professional life comes from creating a successful group of private schools to offer an affordable high-quality alternative...That Mr. Luddy exists is reason enough to believe all is not lost for America."

ROSS KAMINSKY
COLUMNIST, THE AMERICAN SPECTATOR

"Bob Luddy has written the perfect guidebook for young entrepreneurs. It is readable, concise, practical, and relevant, and it reflects Luddy's persistence, business acumen, common sense, and integrity. Every aspiring entrepreneur should read and re-read it."

GARLAND S. TUCKER III
RETIRED CHAIRMAN/CEO, TRIANGLE CAPITAL CORPORATION;
SCHOLAR, JOHN LOCKE FOUNDATION

"A compelling story of entrepreneurial success starting from the germ of an idea to a successful company brought about through hard work, decisive action, innovation, and strong moral values. Bob Luddy's approach to doing business is a great example of how entrepreneurs improve our lives through serving consumers, workers, and suppliers. Definitely an important economic lesson that many need to hear."

DR. STEPHAN F. GOHMANN
DIRECTOR, JOHN H. SCHNATTER CENTER FOR FREE ENTERPRISE;
PROFESSOR OF ECONOMICS, UNIVERSITY OF LOUISVILLE

"Bob Luddy has written a serious how-to book for every aspiring young entrepreneur, illuminating both the technological and character aspects of successful business leadership...It should head the reading list for every school of business."

DR. DONALD J. DEVINE
SENIOR SCHOLAR, THE FUND FOR AMERICAN STUDIES;
PRESIDENT RONALD REAGAN'S FIRST TERM DIRECTOR OF THE U.S. OFFICE
OF PERSONNEL MANAGEMENT

"Robert L. Luddy is a great American, a great entrepreneur, and he understands both economics and education."

DR. TYLER COWEN
PROFESSOR OF ECONOMICS, GEORGE MASON UNIVERSITY;
DIRECTOR, MERCATUS CENTER

August 10, 2018

ENTREPRENEURIAL LIFE

THE PATH FROM STARTUP TO MARKET LEADER

Bob Luddy

ROBERT L. LUDDY

Copy editors: Elaine Klonicki, Holly Wiggin, Cindy Brody
Cover photo: Cameron Powell | Cover design: MODE

www.captiveaire.com

This book is dedicated to my friend and mentor,
Dr. William H. Peterson, who studied under
Ludwig von Mises, one of the great Austrian Economists.

ACKNOWLEDGEMENTS

I would like to thank the following people for their assistance in writing this book: Dr. Bill Peterson, Elaine Klonicki, Holly Wiggin, Tonya Beauchaine, George Leef, Trey Garrison, Cindy Brody, Bill Francis, Judy Nunnenkamp, Harry Silletti, Dr. Myra McCrickard, Dr. Stephen Gohmann, Dr. Gary Klonicki, Whitney Chambers, and Dan Courtney.

I especially appreciate the support of my wife, Maria Luddy, my children, Randy Luddy and Julie Luddy Roach, and my son-in-law Michael Roach.

TO THE DEDICATED EMPLOYEES
OF CAPTIVEAIRE

Leaders are critical and necessary to grow organizations, but an adroit team of dedicated, motivated employees is the lynchpin to growth.

I would like to thank the employees of CaptiveAire for their loyalty, hard work, and dedication to this company over the last forty-plus years. The success of CaptiveAire is due to the relentless pursuit of excellence by each and every one of you. I am proud of our accomplishments, and I look forward to the continued success of both our company and the individuals who make up the CaptiveAire family.

TABLE OF CONTENTS

PART II

ENTREPRENEURIAL MANAGEMENT

ENTREPRENEURIAL LIFE

FOREWORD

As an economist, attorney, and academic—and, more to the point, as the daughter of the man to whom this book is dedicated—I commend it to your attention. I add some of the highest praise I can offer: Dad, who reviewed hundreds of books for The Wall Street Journal's "Reading for Business" column, would have loved it. I only wish that he could have read it.

While Dad was, for most of his working life, a professor, he always admired entrepreneurs. Economic and business literature is replete with references to the entrepreneur, yet for the most part he remains something of a stick figure there. What Bob does in this book is to bring that stick figure to life.

An economist and political scientist who did "get" entrepreneurs is the Austrian-born American Joseph Schumpeter. He pioneered and popularized the concept of "creative destruction," seeing in the entrepreneur "the person who destroys the existing economic order by introducing new products and services, by creating new forms of organization, or by exploiting new raw materials." Or as Bob puts it, "we force ourselves to think disruptively, continually asking ourselves how we can improve the industry in ways previously not considered."

Bob, the consummate entrepreneur, started his own business as a solo proprietor with only $1,300 in savings. He describes here how he built CaptiveAire into the leading national manufacturer of commercial kitchen ventilation systems, with 1,200 employees, six manufacturing plants, one hundred sales offices, and fifty display centers, and with a doubling of sales every five years over the past twenty years. He talks, too, of how he became an educational entrepreneur, opening a public charter school, an independent Catholic high school, and the Thales Academy chain of private, secular college preparatory schools for all grade levels.

Bob doesn't just tell this story, though, as a narrative of events but explains the rationale for his decisions. He discusses, among other things, product redesigns to improve quality and performance and to reduce costs, the introduction of the first assembly line to produce commercial kitchen hoods, and the marketing idea that shook up the industry: the opening of display centers where products are demonstrated, tests are performed, and real-time performance data are generated.

Notably absent from Bob's book is any apparent concern for purely material gain. The driving force for Bob's entrepreneurship is, instead, the constant search for opportunities, which he has repeatedly seized, to solve problems: to improve practices, processes, technologies, products, services, and lead times. It has not been as important to him to be a successful person as to be a valuable person.

Bob has long recognized that learning is part and parcel of entrepreneurship. Learning should, in his view, extend well beyond earning a degree, especially in a dynamic and fast-paced business world; it should involve a never-ending process of intellectual curiosity and engagement. As he so well puts it, "we must...learn how to learn."

Bob's own sources of learning are extensive and varied and include my father, who was a close friend and mentor of his. He credits Dad with helping him to master such important economic concepts as (to name a few) opportunity cost, transaction costs, and comparative advantage.

Each of Bob's chapters opens with a well-chosen quote. My favorite of these quotes is from Henry Adams: "A teacher affects eternity. He can never tell where his influence stops." The quote is apt for Dad but it is also apt for Bob, who is a great teacher as well as a great learner. There are valuable lessons in this book for all businesspeople, especially for those who dream of starting or managing their own business. Each of the chapters in the second half of his book, on entrepreneurial management, closes with several "key takeaways." To cite just one, "reject the status quo and conventional thinking in order to grow."

Bob has himself been a mentor to employees and students, and has endowed, in honor of my father, the Peterson-Luddy Chair in Austrian Economics at the Mises Institute. What Chaucer said of the Clerk of Oxford in *The Canterbury Tales* could equally be said not just of my own father, but of Bob: "And gladly would he learn, and gladly teach." Much can indeed be learned from this fine and remarkable book.

LAURA BENNETT PETERSON, ESQ.
DAUGHTER OF DR. WILLIAM H. PETERSON

Commercial kitchen ventilation is quite technical in nature. This basic explanation of the workings of a typical ventilation system is presented as a reference.

KITCHEN VENTILATION SYSTEM OVERVIEW

A commercial kitchen ventilation system functions to remove cooking fumes, excess hot air, grease, and smoke from a building. The hot fumes from the cooking appliances are captured by the exhaust hood and travel first through the grease filters, which act as a fire barrier while removing some of the grease particles from the airstream. The air then moves through the grease ductwork and out of the building through an exhaust fan that is typically located on the roof of the building.

All air removed from the space must be replaced to maintain proper airflow and building pressure. A make-up air unit, also typically located on the roof of the building, takes outside air and supplies it to the building, sometimes tempering it before sending it through the HVAC duct. The make-up air then enters the hood through a perforated supply plenum, beginning the ventilation cycle once again.

Given the high risk of fire, commercial kitchen ventilation systems also include fire detection and suppression equipment. These systems can be thought of as sprinkler systems located inside the hood, extinguishing fire on the cooktop or within the duct and plenum (area located behind the filters).

Other elements of the kitchen ventilation system include: vertical end panels which act as fire barriers to contain the fire under the hood; utility distribution systems which simplify the utility hook-up process and make appliance layout customization easier; pollution control units which remove odors, smoke, and grease before exhausting air from the building; and cloud-based building management systems which monitor equipment 24/7 and allow for remote adjustment and diagnosis.

Commercial kitchen systems can be relatively basic, or very complex. They are designed based on the size, type, and temperature of cooking equipment, as well as the specific needs of each individual customer. A well-designed system is energy efficient and works in conjunction with the building HVAC system to save on energy costs.

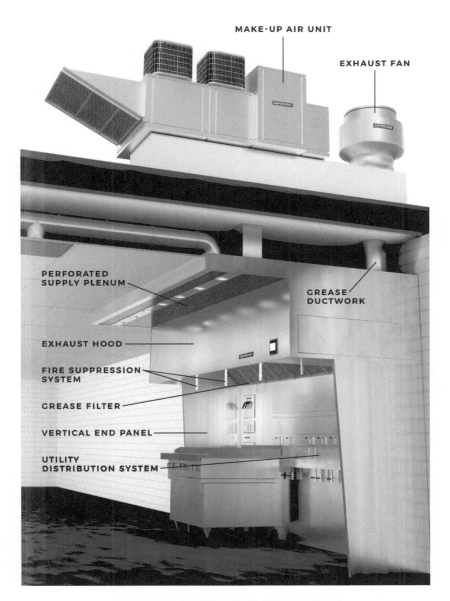

MAKE-UP AIR UNIT

EXHAUST FAN

PERFORATED
SUPPLY PLENUM

GREASE
DUCTWORK

EXHAUST HOOD

FIRE SUPPRESSION
SYSTEM

GREASE FILTER

VERTICAL END PANEL

UTILITY
DISTRIBUTION SYSTEM

CAPTIVEAIRE KITCHEN VENTILATION DIAGRAM

INTRODUCTION

Entrepreneurship is not for everyone. It's a long, hard road. It requires a strong sense of where you're going, coupled with the confidence to take major risks without being overly fearful of the outcome. The commitment and energy required alone deters many hopefuls. It takes a certain type of personality to be able to put yourself voluntarily through so many challenges for such an extended period of time.

Despite the challenges, it's an exciting life, filled with limitless opportunities, and I couldn't imagine doing anything else. The rewards are many, not the least of which is the intrinsic joy of watching an idea come to fruition. It's almost like parenting, in a way. You spend years raising and developing your child and watching it grow. In my case, that "child" evolved to become CaptiveAire Systems, now the largest commercial kitchen ventilation company in North America.

People often ask me how I built my company and became a business leader and educator. Many of these individuals see my current success and think I must have won the luck of the draw in life. What they don't see are the stressful nights in the initial years, when I wondered if we could meet payroll that month. Or the long days marked by complex problems that made my brain hurt from the sheer effort of thinking through them. Or the countless times when I've had to make decisions without having any idea what the right answer was.

Even though the journey has been grueling at times, I wouldn't have it any other way. Entrepreneurs are addicted to the challenge. If it were easy, we'd be bored. Most people try to be comfortable and happy in life. I find my fulfillment in overcoming hardships and persevering to accomplish a goal. I'm competitive, and never satisfied. If we meet a sales goal, it's a temporary high, and then I'm ready to charge after the next one. I think athletes can relate to me on this—winning a game only provides brief satisfaction before you're ready to take on the next contender.

That said, we know that our personal determination can only go so far. Our success also lies largely on the many skills and talents of the individuals we meet and work with along the way. Throughout my life, I've been blessed by the counsel of several mentors, who have shaped and guided my company and me. The most important of these individuals was Dr. Bill Peterson. He was my friend, consultant, and personal professor for over twenty years. A brilliant thinker, teacher, and writer, "Dr. Bill," as I called him, was a lifelong believer in entrepreneurship as critical to economic growth and job creation.

We shared a unique, complimentary relationship—that of the economic theorist and the entrepreneur. During the course of our friendship, until his passing in 2012, he called regularly to ask how I was doing, and to share a joke or anecdote. Our conversations were both stimulating and inspiring. He was an active participant in CaptiveAire's growth, primarily as our economic advisor.

This book was Dr. Peterson's idea. He nurtured the concept, encouraged me in my writing, and prodded me regularly to complete it. Although each entrepreneur has his or her own story, he felt that the elements that led to the success of CaptiveAire could inform others with similar aspirations. I am enormously grateful for the impact Dr.

Peterson had on my life. He wanted me to carry on his work after his departure, which I do with great pleasure and determination.

My entrepreneurial life began at a very early age. By age nine, I had already discovered that I greatly preferred work over school. This revelation set the pattern for the remainder of my life. Throughout my youth I had numerous jobs that were fun, profitable, and built my self-confidence. I began telling everyone I knew that someday I'd own my own business. In my teens I began purchasing stock, and by age twenty I co-owned a small fiberglass company. Each of these experiences prepared me to establish CaptiveAire in my early thirties.

I've been running CaptiveAire for over four decades now, and I've founded several Pre-K-12 schools as well. At this point in my life, while still deeply involved in my business and my schools, I also look to the future and hope to inspire a new generation of entrepreneurs and free market advocates. Here, then, is the story of CaptiveAire, the factors that have led to its growth, and some of the philosophies I've found useful in my time at the helm. I hope it provides value to you.

PART ONE

THE HISTORY OF CAPTIVEAIRE

"The best way to predict the future is to create it."

PETER DRUCKER

CHAPTER ONE

CULTIVATING
THE ENTREPRENEUR

Denial was no longer possible. I was forced to face the frightening reality: We would not be able to meet the monthly payroll. All my thoughts and actions had been focused on doing everything possible to postpone this failure and find a way to survive. In situations like this, the solutions are never obvious; all I had to rely on was my own grit and determination.

It was June 30, 1980, when my options ran out. I informed our eighteen employees at Atlantic Fire Systems, Inc., that payroll would be delayed due to technical issues. I offered a small advance to anyone with a hardship, which I drew from the meager funds available. Our monthly payroll was on the 30th of each month. We had the entire month to collect our accounts receivable, but it did not work out that June because we had a very poor collections month. In fact, we had only a few thousand dollars in the bank to meet a $30,000 payroll demand.

A reduction of our team was the only option at that point. It was a tough decision, but once I realized it was the only viable one, I downsized our staff immediately. When you have to make a decision like that—meeting the reality of market conditions—it is imperative that you do not hesitate. Decisions of this nature are always made boldly and implemented quickly and without regret for what might have been. It is one of the reasons the company survived many crises over time. Crisis management is something I learned first during my small jobs as a teenager, and later throughout my professional experiences.

After a difficult first and second quarter for the economy and for Atlantic Fire Systems, Inc., I was not certain we would survive the third quarter of the year. It was a difficult time for everyone in business. The economic recessions of the 1970s caused sluggish growth and high inflation in the early 1980s. It was also difficult to collect accounts receivable, which exacerbated cash flow.

I struggled with two competing thoughts. The first: "Failure is inevitable." The second: "I cannot and will not fail." My whole life had provided me with the skills to deal with difficult situations, but I had reached the point where entrepreneurial grit becomes imperative. Many problems are daunting; my job was to find solutions.

EARLY LIFE

I grew up in Harrisburg, Pennsylvania, in a large family of eight children. My father was an engineer for the Pennsylvania Railroad and my mother was busy full time raising the family. We had great joy together but very little money. My grandparents lived nearby and influenced my siblings and me as they were born in the late nineteenth century and were steeped in the American traditions of church, family, education, and hard work.

My maternal grandfather was a partner in a men's clothing store called "Westfall's," in Altoona, Pennsylvania. He began working in the early 1900s and was successful because of his people skills and business acumen. By the time he retired in 1950, he had acquired fifty percent of the stock in the company and its retail building. He encouraged my siblings and me to find jobs early, as he believed in the lessons they taught regarding how one should interact with people. He was delighted to share his business experiences and knowhow.

My father was a mathematician, machinist, and self-taught engineer. His hours working for the Pennsylvania Railroad were long. He was in management, which sometimes required him to cover two shifts. His work ethic was a great example for me, as he had great pride in his work and performance.

Dad and his five brothers all went to college in the 1930s and '40s. It was expected that my siblings and I would do the same. A life-long learner before that cliché became popular, he read everything from newspapers to electronics magazines.

Dad was proud of his ability to build or fix anything. He was skilled at woodworking, wiring, and plumbing, and he could repair TVs, washing machines, and cars. He even built additional rooms in our house as our family expanded.

In my family, debates were encouraged, but lasting disagreements were not acceptable. Dad was an impressive thinker and debater. He could maintain either side of an argument and simply enjoyed the exchange. As youngsters we participated, learning verbal skills and logic, both of which proved to be very valuable.

Dad placed a very high value on family and this included the extended family on both sides. We still gather together often for reunions. Our countryside home is used for major holidays and other celebrations; family members and friends are always welcome.

Mother was an optimistic and joyful homemaker. Even into her late nineties, she bound the family together and continued to remind us of the values she instilled in us. She was a voracious reader who preferred biographies to fiction, especially those of the Founding Fathers and others who have excelled in life. When I was growing up, Mother often talked about her brother, my Uncle Bill Courtney, who became an entrepreneur by opening a cup vending business just after World War II. The company flourished and later merged into Servomation, which became a national NYSE company. His story and others like it were what inspired me to join the ranks of entrepreneurs.

Our mother's trust in our judgment allowed my siblings and me to mature quickly. In effect, she taught us some of the early tools of entrepreneurship. She instilled in us common sense ideas and the importance of working hard and being resourceful. We all had jobs early on in life. Beginning in elementary school, I babysat, shoveled snow, and worked a paper route. My sisters baked cookies, sewed clothes, and also babysat. We were encouraged to be active, and we were praised for our accomplishments. I chose to save my money and invest it in items such as a home movie camera to make videos of the family.

FIRST JOBS

One Friday afternoon, at age eleven, I announced to my mother that I had just secured a job working on a bread delivery truck every Saturday. Her response was, "Bobby, you are too young." I informed her that I had already made a commitment and I really wanted the job. My mother was our family disciplinarian, moral compass, and first teacher. In light of my determination, she supported my plan. She was like that—protective—but she encouraged us to push ourselves and to use our judgment well. For my work I received $4 a day and was able to bring home a surplus of sweet rolls and loaves of bread for the family. I also sold greeting cards and brought in a small income with that pursuit.

The basic lessons I learned at a young age are the concepts every successful venture is built on: to show up on time, be courteous, do a thorough job, and make sure the customer is happy.

When I was hired to deliver prescriptions and stock shelves at the local drug store at the age of fifteen, I valued my job and the opportunity to be involved in a real business. The owner, Dr. Galen Bayer, taught me the basics of running a small company, including retail sales, inventory stocking and ordering, cash management, and customer relations. I was learning and getting paid—only eighty-five cents per hour—but the reality was that I should have been paying him for the rich experience.

The earnings and savings were important to me, but more important was learning how the world worked and how to deal with people and handle money. Some of my friends told me I would never enjoy life if I spent all of my time working, but they didn't understand that I loved these jobs. I was thrilled to learn the ins and outs of business at a very young age.

While other kids were reading comic books and sports almanacs, I was learning how to read stock tables. Our next-door neighbor, Dr. Tilman Foust, a radiologist, provided me copies of his *Wall Street Journal* and taught me about investments. I learned how the ticker tape ran and read about major companies and their potential.

When I was sixteen, I used $500 of the money I had saved to purchase my first shares of stock at the investment firm Walston & Company. I had selected twenty shares of Pennsylvania Power and Light (PPL), but the broker had to call my mother for permission since I was a minor. My parents had never been in the market themselves, so the broker had to assure Mother it was a good choice before she signed for me. I was hooked and have been involved in the stock market ever since.

In 1963, I graduated from Bishop McDevitt High School. Concurrently, my father took a new job and the family moved to Philadelphia. This was a big change from the smaller town of Harrisburg. In Philadelphia, I had the opportunity to attend a well-known, affordable college, LaSalle College (now University). I majored in Corporate Finance, a curriculum that seemed tailor-made for me.

LaSalle is a unique, Catholic institution, founded by the Christian Brothers who have over 300 years of teaching experience. In the early '60s, LaSalle was an all-male college, and most of us came from working-class families. Many of us commuted daily. The academic environment was rigorous, with classes including finance, accounting, law, mathematics, and investments; but also well-rounded, incorporating philosophy, logic, and liberal arts as well. The Christian Brothers wanted our education to be wide-ranging, so they worked hard to develop us as future leaders and thinkers.

On the first day in his accounting class, Brother Phillip told us that there were three primary requirements to pass his class. We were expected to thoroughly understand generally accepted accounting principles, standard accounting methods and, finally, fiduciary responsibility. I have always remembered these important concepts because Brother Phillip made them part of our daily instruction.

Another of my teachers, Professor Dan Rodden, imparted a gem of wisdom that my peers and I did not grasp at the time. Today, I often repeat Professor Rodden's daily directive to "order the disordered." His philosophy was that life is disordered, and it's up to us to create order from chaos.

While attending LaSalle, I officially became an entrepreneur, using my savings to buy into a small fiberglass manufacturing business called "Uni-Form Fiberglass," with a partner. We made boats, radome covers (structural protective enclosures), pump housings, and all types of reinforced fiberglass products. It was a difficult business—the product was messy and hard to control. We struggled for financing, barely meeting payroll, but made consistent progress until I completed college. (Incidentally, I observed a sheet metal operation nearby and to my mind, it appeared to be a simpler business. Years later, when the opportunity arose to get into the hood manufacturing business, I was convinced it was a better choice in that it offered the opportunity to produce highly predictable results in terms of quality and cost.)

ARMY LIFE

In the summer of 1967, my military deferment expired and I was drafted into the Army, which required the sale of the fiberglass business. I received a short extension in order to complete the sale, and in January of 1968 I entered the U.S. Army for a two-year hitch beginning with basic training at Fort Bragg in North Carolina.

The Army basic infantry training was tough, but I learned some critical lessons that still guide me today. The most important was humanity's great capacity for physical and mental endurance. These are crucial traits for entrepreneurs, as life's undertakings always take longer and are more difficult than first envisioned.

After completion of advanced infantry training, I was assigned to Fort Carson, Colorado, and then later to Tent City B, near Saigon, Vietnam, in the finance division.

During my two years of service, I realized that it is possible to adapt to most conditions when required. Such experiences provide valuable lessons for developing character and judgment. I also learned that we all have much higher capabilities than routinely used. Later, when I faced complex challenges, somehow they became easier because of my military experience. Following my tenure in Vietnam, I was discharged from the Army at Travis Air Force Base near San Francisco on January 9, 1970, more than ready to return to civilian life.

OPPORTUNITIES AWAIT

Early in 1970, a former associate in Philadelphia offered me a job in Los Angeles working as the finance controller at a fiberglass manufacturing plant. He was the majority partner but the minority partners operated the business. They were very shrewd Armenians. I quickly learned how to operate in a challenging environment, representing the financial interest of the majority shareholder. After a year, I decided to move on and became a manufacturer's representative, selling fiberglass components such as brick panels and decorative fireplace surrounds for new homes and mobile homes. This afforded me the opportunity to learn about the construction industry, which proved to be a huge asset.

In 1974, I resolved to make a change. I was married by then, and I was tired of the traffic and congestion in Los Angeles. I did some research about the areas of the country most likely to grow economically in the coming decades, and from those I chose North Carolina. We moved to Raleigh, the capital city, with some savings, but no contacts or job leads.

There was a recession at the time, due to the high gas prices from the Arab oil crisis. (OPEC had imposed an oil embargo the previous year, which seriously disrupted supply.) Jobs were scarce, but I applied for every one listed in the newspaper. One day a man named Phil Ellington called and asked if I was interested in selling fire and safety equipment. Persistence paid off—I was selected and began selling automatic dry chemical fire suppression systems to restaurants. This was a lucky break, and I made the most of it.

After two years I was fairly well compensated and we were able to purchase our first home. However, at a weekend sales meeting in Atlanta in 1976, the CEO informed us that the company was not doing well financially. Our pay would be reduced by about one third, which I found unacceptable.

A FATEFUL DECISION

Returning home that Sunday, I began to realize that perhaps the time had come to start my own business. We all like ample time to make decisions, but in the entrepreneurial world, decisions must be made quickly. Once a decision is made, there's no point agonizing, worrying, or dithering about it. It was time to act.

I decided to open a similar type of business, focused on selling and installing fire suppression systems in restaurants. I had only $1,300 in savings and no way to obtain the Ansul components I would need for the business. (Ansul is the dominant manufacturer of restaurant fire systems.) I did not waste time looking for more capital, but used the Milton Friedman approach of sweat capital, which means you build capital with earnings from hard work. As Ross Perot says, "Brains, insight, and creativity are incredible substitutes for capital."

My mother taught us to do things right away rather than procrastinate; her constant refrain was "Tomorrow never comes." I decided to persevere against the odds and informed my boss, Phil Ellington, of my decision to leave the company. He was one of the great men I have been privileged to know and he was very understanding.

This illustrates a key entrepreneurial lesson. There are times when you know the right answer, but you can't fully defend it with logical arguments, and certainly not with spreadsheets. Sometimes it's just instinctive, and you have to go with your gut. This was clearly one of those cases.

Our minds are able to process more information than we are consciously aware of, and I'm convinced that's where our gut feelings come from, at least in regard to higher concepts and complex ideas. My biggest mistakes have occurred when I let someone talk me into something that went against my gut instinct. Learning to understand and trust your gut is an ongoing process of expanding your knowledge and honing your skills. I believe this is why entrepreneurs and pioneers are so put off by committees, leadership by consensus, and the entire bureaucratic method.

The early acquired education, work ethic, and understanding of the value of money helped form me into an entrepreneur. The support of my family and the values they instilled were my guiding light. Early experiences gave me a desire to make my mark on the world and I felt the pull to put my knowledge to the test as an entrepreneur.

"The secret of success is constancy to purpose."

BENJAMIN FRANKLIN

CHAPTER TWO

OPEN FOR BUSINESS 1976–1982

Five days after that fateful Sunday sales meeting, on November 1, 1976, I was in business for myself. I was thirty-one years old, with a growing family. Our daughter, Julie, had been born in March of that year, so the stakes were high. Within forty-eight hours I had opened a bank account and purchased supplies and equipment. To save time, I converted our home phone number to a business line, and to save money, I worked out of our garage.

I gave some real thought to the name for my new company. I wanted it to appear first in its category in the phone book. I decided "Atlantic Fire Systems, Inc." would be a fitting name for a company located just two hours from the Atlantic Ocean, smack dab in the middle of Atlantic Coast Conference territory. I began the process of forming a corporation with name registration, obtained a tax ID number, and had some business cards printed. My attorney commented that someday this might be a large corporation, and these turned out to be very prophetic words.

The major obstacles to the startup included locating a supplier for the Ansul fire suppression systems and finding working capital. Ansul products were sold through a relatively small number of distributors, and my former employer was the distributor for the Carolinas and Georgia. Fortunately, a friend named Johnny Turner operated a small fire system service company, and he purchased the Ansul products for me out of state. Johnny was a lifesaver and his assistance was critical to my early success.

The severe lack of capital presented a major obstacle, but I wouldn't allow it to keep me from trying to succeed in this new business. Samuel Johnson once said, "Nothing will ever be attempted if all possible objections must first be overcome." The personal risk was high, but I was determined.

Fortunately, most of my former customers followed me to my new venture. From the beginning, I knew that low prices and fast service would be the cornerstones of growth. This was proven late one evening during Christmas week when a restaurant owner in Chapel Hill called me. He said they had an inspection the next day and needed help with some modifications to their fire system. Without hesitation I agreed and drove an hour to his restaurant to make the repairs. The appreciative owner became one of my best marketing agents, telling everyone he knew about Atlantic Fire Systems. This turned out to be a valuable lesson for me, as our primary marketing tool until very recently has always been word of mouth.

Around the same time, a good friend of mine started in the same type of business, but it took him more than six months to launch his company. He lost valuable time and resources in the process. Eight months later he was out of business because he had used up all of his capital during the lethargic startup. When you're in business for yourself, you must be quick. When I was at Fort Bragg's bayonet school, they taught us about two types of fighters: "the quick and the dead." I've found this to be a helpful metaphor for business.

OFF TO A GOOD START

The initial months went well for Atlantic Fire Systems, but by January of 1977, I could no longer handle both the selling and the installing. I was doing as much as I could as a sole proprietor. It became necessary to hire my first employee, much earlier than anticipated. It was going to put a strain on cash flow because we were in that middle ground between too much work for one person and not enough revenue to cover two employees. Around that time, an installer who worked for my former employer contacted me for a job. I knew he had excellent skills and would be a good fit. Business was growing rapidly and the addition of our first full-time installer dramatically increased capacity.

I moved out of my garage and into a small office building nearby on Duraleigh Road, with a front room for my desk, typewriter, and phone, and a back room to store the equipment necessary for the installations. It was bare bones, but it served its purpose.

My first big break occurred in March of 1977, five months after opening. Ansul decided to add a second restaurant systems distributor in North Carolina. The Ansul factory sales representative contacted me and offered to appoint Atlantic Fire Systems as an official distributor. It meant we would receive the best pricing and some national installation business, which was important for sales growth.

During this first year, we began to install kitchen exhaust hoods as well as fire systems, which generated new customers and revenue. This broadened our appeal, but meant that we had to develop new skills and buy more equipment. The expansion of our services involved formidable obstacles such as deciphering building codes, learning new welding methods, and figuring out how to install different mechanical equipment. As I quickly realized, entrepreneurs are faced with an onslaught of problems every day. The process of learning to navigate challenges swiftly builds confidence and solidifies capabilities.

In the late 1970s, local sheet metal shops, kitchen equipment fabricators, and a small number of national or regional manufacturers were the primary makers of commercial kitchen hoods. The hoods were sometimes crudely constructed with inconsistent welds and rough edges that cut the hands of the cooks who tried to clean them.

In addition, the fabricators were not highly knowledgeable about the science of air movement, which is critical to the design of kitchen systems. Exhaust flow rates were high, consuming too much energy; kitchen hoods were not very reliable; and the available systems did not address creature comfort. In simple terms, restaurant kitchens were hot, greasy, and uncomfortable. Kitchen ventilation was a slow-moving industry at that time, with many products below the threshold of quality needed for modern restaurants.

Meanwhile, the national manufacturers charged very high prices, beyond what small restaurant owners could afford. Over time it became obvious that kitchen ventilation represented a major opportunity for my fledgling company, if I could keep my costs low enough to create an affordable line of highly effective products.

EXPANDED HORIZONS

It is rare to have two major breaks in one year, but it happened when Golden Corral awarded Atlantic Fire a contract to supply and install all of their kitchen ventilation systems. The initial order was over $40,000, which constituted thirteen percent of the entire sales revenue for 1977. (Sales for the year were just shy of $300,000, much higher than my rough prediction of $75,000.) With this order, we gained experience and learned contracting skills, and more importantly, our users now recognized Atlantic Fire as a quality supplier.

Golden Corral became more than an important customer; it was our flagship account, which we leveraged to win many new national accounts. I knew the owners and operating officers well, and we did everything possible to serve and create value for this rapidly growing chain. I hired my youngest brother, Mike, to lead the installation crew for this contract, and he proved to be a valuable member of our team. I constantly reminded my employees how important it was to maintain this business over the long haul. Golden Corral is still one of our best accounts.

In 1978, after realizing the shortcomings of the kitchen hoods we'd been purchasing from vendors (welding and performance issues), my brother and I decided we could produce these hoods ourselves. We had no equipment and limited knowledge as to how to go about it. Initially, we thought it might make sense to have another company bend the metal before we welded the hoods together. But it turned out that the complexity of bending hoods all but precluded this initial plan of ours. Metal dies could only bend defined angles such as ninety or forty-five degrees, but we needed a larger number of varying angles to support our designs.

We theorized about the best way to bend hood panels, but the technology needed to meet our requirements did not exist yet. We were able to get a few fabricated hood panels made, but the equipment we were using had severe limitations in length and gauges. Initially, because of our inexperience, we didn't think the job would be that difficult. As we proceeded, we began to realize the incredible challenges of design and manufacturing.

EARLY-STAGE CAPABILITIES

One day in the spring of 1978, I received an unexpected call from Benn Maynard, the father of Golden Corral co-founder James Maynard, who was their company's construction manager. He asked me to meet him at a small sheet metal shop nearby. At our rendezvous, Benn suggested that I needed a shop for my work and informed me that this shop, owned by one of Golden Corral's failing suppliers, was for sale. I inquired how much it would cost and he said that the price was $1,600. I didn't have the money, and told him so. He replied simply, "You'll figure out how to make it work."

I realized that he was conscious of what I needed and was providing his help gratuitously. Taking this step was crucial, so I squeezed out the funds from our meager cash flow and purchased the shop. It was a risky move, but this would prove to be the decision that would change the course and long-term direction of the company. Earlier that year, we also rented a slightly larger office space—a small house in an area of Raleigh called Oak Park.

After these transactions, my brother Mike began to focus his energies on making hoods. Soon enough it became obvious to me that I didn't have time to make hoods and run the fire systems business. I sold the shop to him, and he renamed it Luddy Sheet Metal.

Mike had very strong technical skills and was a hard worker. He hired Herbert McCoy, one of our sub-contractors who knew how to make commercial stainless steel kitchen hoods, to teach him everything he knew. Mike also purchased a Roto-Dye which was a metal bender designed to work with light gauge sheet metal. Over the next few years, Mike developed the early-stage capabilities of basic hoods, which I sold through Atlantic Fire Systems. At the same time, we also purchased hoods from another manufacturer named Grease Master in Charlotte, North Carolina.

The following year, in 1979, we came up with an exclusive trade name for our hoods, as we realized how important branding was. Ironically, our name came from something negative in the news, which we were able to turn into a positive. One night our independent sales representative was watching news reports on the Iranian hostage crisis about the Americans held captive in Iran. Since kitchen hoods are primarily designed to capture and remove smoke and cooking effluents (grease and gasses that are produced), the name "CaptiveAire" came to his mind. We liked it and began using it. In 1981, we filed for a national trademark, and it was granted on October 12, 1982.

In August of 1979, our son Randy was born. The fire equipment business was running well by then; Atlantic Fire achieved sales of one million dollars that year, our third year in business. The two key factors in achieving this fast growth were the Ansul distributorship and the major contract from Golden Corral. We moved again, this time into a small industrial area in West Raleigh called Umstead Industrial Park. We rented a building that had both office space and a warehouse area. With our name on the park sign, we began to feel like a real company.

MR. BILL AND THE "SILVER FOXES"

After my father, Bill Luddy, retired, he began helping me part time, as he had the engineering and technical skills we desperately needed. He helped Atlantic Fire qualify for another distributorship with Ansul: this one for Halon, a fire-fighting chemical used in rooms housing mainframe computer equipment. The Halon product line allowed us to expand into the light commercial fire protection business.

In his seventies, "Mr. Bill," as he was affectionately called by the staff, recruited some of his friends, who were also retired engineers. They came to work for us on a part-time basis, helping with quality and safety issues. These seasoned men were known around the company as the "silver foxes." They provided the benefit of many years of experience, established our quality control program and electrical controls division, and improved our manufacturing processes. If anyone violated the standards, Dad would provide a short, pointed lecture on the importance of quality.

Through their efforts we were able to implement policies that brought decades of experience to a company only a few years old. My father also wrote a software selection program named CASPER that facilitated accurate information for production. This information included duct sizes and locations, the number of lights, length and width of the hood, and notes for special requirements. Fan data included voltage and motor phase along with the model, which contained the diameter of the fan wheel. The data generated from CASPER included all of the information needed by manufacturing to produce the hoods and fans, thereby expediting the production process.

Dad was involved in electrical controls design on a regular basis. He essentially established our electrical engineering design department. His influence left an indelible mark on CaptiveAire. Although my father passed away in 1996, his presence is still felt and his guidance is still present throughout our company.

The early 1980s were financially challenging, with high interest rates and slow growth, as the country experienced the pains of a recession. Atlantic Fire had too much debt because of the fast growth and a weak capital base in the preceding years. In June 1980, the company hit its low point—the frightening moment when I realized I could not meet payroll that began this story. I was confronted with the possibility that the company might fail or go bankrupt.

I'd done everything humanly possible to save the company, so now all that remained was the grace of God. As a man of faith, in critical situations like this, when I had done all else possible, I prayed. Everything good we do is because of God's grace. He expects us to help ourselves, but sometimes, we need a little extra help.

The following Monday night I stopped by the company's post office box and found a check from Golden Corral for $28,000, almost the exact amount I needed to make the delayed payroll. I'm not saying for certain that there was divine intervention, but you can bet I gave thanks to God and to Golden Corral, in that order, and breathed a sigh of relief. We had dodged a bullet, but due to very slow collections, I had to make that difficult decision to lay off several employees for the first time.

By 1981, my brother Mike had developed an interest in computers and wanted to pursue programming. He sold Luddy Sheet Metal back to Atlantic Fire Systems and went on to start another company, POSITRAK, which produced a point-of-sale computer system for auto parts companies. I now had to manage both Luddy Sheet Metal and Atlantic Fire, the latter of which was struggling due to excessive interest rates. I began for the first time to seek some bank financing to stabilize the company. However, it became apparent that my first contacts did not see the company as bankable.

FOCUSING ON THE FINANCES

Fortunately, the Southern National Bank of North Carolina had a financing division which made loans supported by accounts receivable. In the summer of 1981, I was able to negotiate a $300,000 loan to pay off our short-term debts. The interest payments were at an astounding twenty-four percent, prime rate plus four percent. As much as I hated to borrow, this loan was imperative for survival.

The bank loan covenants required me to hire a chief financial officer. I was reluctant but placed an ad in the local paper, *The News & Observer*. I hoped to find someone competent who would be able to handle the complex finances and accounting requirements of a growing company. The best candidate was Bill Francis, who still serves as our CFO today. Bill turned out to be a methodical, skilled money manager. He pored over our books, formalizing our accounting processes and providing me with the detailed financial reports I needed to make important decisions. On his first day, I handed Bill a laundry list of major problems to be solved. Two years later he handed the list back to me: mission accomplished.

In 1981, I also began to hire regional sales managers to aid our continuous expansion, which turned out to be a major game changer. It would reinvigorate the company and put us on track for increased growth. The first regional sales manager was Lonnie Grant, and he opened our initial out-of-town sales office in Greensboro, North Carolina. Lonnie had a strong work ethic and was fiercely determined, and as a result, the sales started trickling in.

Encouraged, I decided to hire four more salespeople that same year, despite the fact that it strained the finances to the limit. I paid them a small base salary, but with their commissions, they had the potential to make a good living. I recruited my brother, Steve Luddy, to open the Wilmington, North Carolina office. He was doing very well selling life insurance with Metropolitan Life at the time and had the sales experience we needed. Steve covered Eastern North and South Carolina, and his was one of the first regions to heavily promote hoods and fans using the trade name CaptiveAire.

Steve was highly instrumental in helping CaptiveAire improve both its product offerings and service record. (He later moved to Florida and opened the first office out of state. This positioned us to secure sales with the Darden restaurant group on his very first sales call. Darden was a major account, which helped accelerate our growth. More than thirty-five years later, it is one of our top five national accounts.)

Dennis Jaynes was initially based in our corporate facilities in Raleigh, but his territory consisted primarily of Virginia. He was one of the first people to recognize that CaptiveAire could become a national manufacturing company. Dennis went on to handle selected accounts and distribution from the western part of our state.

Our fourth representative covered the Raleigh area, and the final one handled our national accounts and franchise business. The new regionals were off to a great start, but we were all still learning, and we hadn't quite figured out the formula. As a result, the volume of sales was not yet consistent. In 1982, after hearing from Bill Francis that we had lost money over the last several months, I took over the job of sales manager. I spent the majority of my time directing our team to increase sales. As a result of my new role, we began to make consistent profits, every month, which was a significant achievement.

Sometimes as a leader you delegate and let your people handle things. But when there's a serious problem, you have to be ready and willing to step in and take over. I always believed this for short-term problems. I never imagined that it would lead to a self-imposed long-term assignment. Except for a few short interludes, I have continued to this day as the leader of the sales teams.

The purchase of the sheet metal shop from Mike and the hiring of the regional sales force marked the beginning of real growth of our kitchen ventilation products. A few months after I took over sales, we had regained profitability. I always managed for the long term but never forgot the importance of making a profit every month to ensure we would be around in the long term.

Our market share was increasing at a rapid pace due to our tenacious sales pioneers. We encouraged them to be as independent as possible, and empowered those in the corporate office to respond to the salespeople's needs quickly so problems could be resolved without delay.

*"Our business in life is not to get ahead of others,
but to get ahead of ourselves—to break our own records,
to outstrip our yesterday by our today."*

STEWART B. JOHNSON

CHAPTER THREE

ROBUST GROWTH 1982–1989

After six arduous years, 1982 proved to be pivotal for CaptiveAire's growth. Our landlord offered to sell us a modern 15,000-square-foot manufacturing plant with no money down, and he financed the building. This agreement was quickly finalized and we moved all operations to Bramer Drive in Raleigh in the fall of 1982. It was perfect for us, with office space up front and a large manufacturing area in the back. This was another huge milestone for CaptiveAire—the purchase of our own building.

Not long afterward, we received a call from a manufacturer's representative for a company named Darley in Maastricht, Holland. The owner had invented a new lightning-fast method of bending metal using computer software with a hydraulic press break. This was a revolutionary process, which reduced die changes and could bend any angle or metal gauge necessary.

We immediately recognized this process as one we had envisioned back in 1978, and literally bought the machine on the spot for $60,000. We didn't have the cash or financing for the purchase, but my view was that this was just another challenge to be resolved. It was a huge investment, but we knew it would allow us to triple production and reduce labor costs significantly. It would also produce very flexible designs, which were necessary to meet challenging customer requirements. CaptiveAire was one of the first companies in America to adopt this technology, which is now the standard of the sheet metal industry worldwide.

In the years to come, we would continue to redefine how hoods were manufactured by emphasizing performance and cost. The supporting technologies for air handling and energy management did not exist. It would be many years before we developed all of the technologies necessary for robust and efficient systems. The road to unlocking the supporting physics and best product ideas would be long and arduous, but ultimately highly rewarding.

AN ENTREPRENEURIAL FAMILY

The balance between family life and career is never perfect or easy, but it is especially challenging for entrepreneurs. Still, children are adaptive, and during Julie and Randy's formative years, I often took them along with me, including evening drop-offs at UPS or the bus station. When Julie was three, she flew with me to Los Angeles. Her grandmother cared for her as I installed hoods and made sales calls.

On Saturdays the kids enjoyed coming to work with me for a few hours, to open the mail and clean up my office. Randy was drawn to tools and showed an early aptitude for construction. The best way to learn how to run a business is to grow up in an entrepreneurial family, as they did. If you start children off early enough, they don't even think of the tasks they're doing as "work," and they learn valuable, confidence-building skills as they mature. CaptiveAire was a huge part of our lives and culture and it was exciting to be sharing it with my children.

LAYING THE GROUNDWORK

One hallmark of successful business owners is that they heed, or at least consider, good advice from other entrepreneurs. In September of 1983, I happened to be flying with Bill Carl, co-founder of Golden Corral, and mentioned that, due to our growth, we needed to hire more people. He suggested that I hire Judy Nunnenkamp, his assistant at the time, to handle our human resources and other administrative tasks. He had retired from the company, so she would be available. I hired Judy, and it turned out to be an inspired decision.

Judy is intuitive, indefatigable, and has extraordinary integrity. Over time, she took on more and more roles until, for a while, she was handling all of the HR, marketing, and plant management with no administrative staff. With a knack for getting the best out of people, she personally mentored most of our employees during the rapid expansion of the 1980s, and went on to become our VP of Human Resources.

By 1984, Bill Francis, our CFO, had garnered the respect and confidence of the bankers on our behalf, and he was able to negotiate a standard bank loan, which paid off our original loan. We were financially stable, due in no small part to Bill's ability to maintain the fine balance between growth and cost control. It had taken eight years to reach consistent profitability, but that's not unusual for startups.

In early 1984, we also executed a major transition and decided to sell off the original fire systems installation business, Atlantic Fire, to focus our full attention on kitchen ventilation. We adopted CaptiveAire as both our trade and corporate name, and registered as Captive-Aire Systems, Inc. (We have dropped the hyphen in recent years.)

The change was profound and critical to our long-term growth. The commercial kitchen ventilation market proved to have virtually unlimited growth potential. We concentrated on it, which allowed us to move toward national sales efforts. That same year we hired four young engineers to help us deal with the various challenges we encountered with our product line as we added diverse customers with specific requirements.

When these inexperienced engineers came on board, one of our salespeople asked why we didn't hire one experienced engineer and save money. My answer was that only limited knowledge was available about commercial kitchen ventilation in general, and most of the great ideas were yet to be discovered.

We were up to fifty employees by then, a point where some companies start to stagnate. I wanted new people who would look at problems with fresh eyes, a concept we've always embraced. As you gain business or technical experience, it's tempting to believe that you have all the right answers. We have always encouraged our employees to speak up and offer radically different solutions than those being discussed. Many of the ideas don't work out, but occasionally someone offers a revolutionary concept—one you had not previously considered. Existing employees are always wary of new hires, but we believe fresh, young blood is good for the company. Their inexperience and willingness to take risks helps us resist the status quo.

We also adopted AutoCAD, a computer assisted drawing program, as our standard engineering software. It seems obvious in today's world, but at the time it was a huge innovation that allowed us to provide drawings and blueprints to users with all of the details they needed. Our competitors did not offer this type of fast service, which afforded us a major competitive edge.

With business growing so rapidly, we desperately needed additional manufacturing space. We expanded the manufacturing area of the Bramer Drive plant, which increased our total square footage there to 23,500.

It was apparent in late 1984 that some of my early team members were the most competent leaders, so I placed my full confidence in them by making them officers of the company. I named Bill Francis to be Vice President of Finance, and my brother Steve to be Vice President of Sales. In 1985, I asked Judy Nunnenkamp to join them as Vice President of Human Resources.

BOLD AND DECISIVE CHOICES

Entrepreneurs make many daring decisions, but they must be well thought out and executed. Sometimes they are so bold that people don't realize how much work went into the planning. Our sales reached $6 million for the year 1985, and we were ranked #65 on the *Inc.* 500 list. I informed our sales force that I had a plan to achieve $25 million in sales within five years. The large sales target was astounding to them at the time. Most of our team dismissed this goal as unattainable, but it became a reality. Steve Luddy was the first to join the millionaires' club (selling one million dollars worth of product in a single year), followed by Lonnie Grant and Dennis Jaynes. In 1986 we reached #43 on the *Inc.* 500 list.

We always tried new ways to improve our services, products, and lead-times, so that same year we opened a specialized plant to produce rooftop equipment such as fans, roof curbs, and air handlers (the outside components of the ventilation system). One of Judy's first new hires in 1983 was a plant supervisor named Cal Heinske. He had done such an effective job for us that we asked him to be the manager of the new plant, which was in a rented warehouse south of Raleigh, near Garner, on Durham Drive. He opened it with a small crew of under ten people, and set new standards for quality, production, and low-cost manufacturing. The production flow was efficient and orderly, and the lead time for production was under five days. Cal turned out to be one of the early influential employees who built CaptiveAire.

In 1986, we achieved only a small sales gain, which was disappointing after four years of robust growth. Our new national accounts sales manager presented a disturbing report to me. He knew my goal was to be a large manufacturer, but he didn't believe that those ambitions could be realized. He tried to convince me that we had pushed our competitors to the bunkers. He thought future sales gains would be very difficult, and we should now take a realistic approach, meaning that we should settle for slower growth.

My first thought was, *"What kind of an accounts manager would waste time writing reports about why we cannot grow?"* His report was contrary to my belief that the company could solve any problem, overcome any obstacle, and beat any competitor. Needless to say, he had a very short career with the company.

Never give up your dream, though others may fail to share or understand it. Establishing and achieving high goals are the essence of a growth company. Playing it safe and settling for average results are not part of my thinking. As CEO and entrepreneur, it is your job to set the standard for the rest of the team. You set a high bar, and everyone else will follow.

Within a year, we had grown large enough to lease a corporate office in a complex called Highwoods in North Raleigh. It was an enormous improvement from the cramped facilities that had previously served as our offices.

RAMPING UP PRODUCTION

Initially our hood manufacturing was done in cells, or welding booths, with each welder assembling and welding sheets of metal into an entire hood in one room. When the hood was fully constructed, it included lights and filters and was ready for shipment. This was a slow process, which could take up to a week for complicated or larger hoods. Over time, some welders were able to produce three hoods per week, which was a major productivity gain.

We also had a layout department, which cut and bent the metal used in the welding booth. We had a small finish department, which installed some electrical switches, did final clean up, and readied the hoods for the shipping department. In the early days, hoods were usually shipped on pallets, often on dedicated trucks or trailers.

We continued using the same process from 1978 until late 1986, when we could no longer produce enough to meet demand. We didn't have the luxury of time to solve this problem. Immediate action was necessary. I was determined to ramp up production by changing the process. I met with two of our young engineers and opened the meeting with this comment: "We are not departing from this room until we have a solution."

Need fosters innovation, and we decided in that meeting to move from the cell system to three distinct processes. A new Pre-Assembly group would cut holes, insulate, and provide some preliminary welding by joining some panels. The welder would then have fewer tasks and would not need to complete the product. A Post-Assembly finish department would install lights, electrical packages, fire systems, and perform the final clean up. As the meeting was wrapping up, I was asked when this new system would be in effect; my quick response was "7:00 a.m. tomorrow morning." The meeting took just ninety minutes.

The implementation process began the next day. We reduced the tasks for our welders and within a few months we increased our production output by fifty percent. We continued with the same setup, with some refinements, for years.

This method of immediate action is important because "doing it now" creates momentum and allows you to reach your goals quickly, without wasting time.

BREAKING AWAY FROM THE PACK

During the Christmas holiday in 1987, I considered the large price increases that were occurring in the stainless steel market. (Stainless steel was our prime raw material.) I had an idea and put together a rough plan to reduce the metal weight while also improving our product, a process often referred to as "lightweighting." Mark Profet, now a successful regional sales manager for CaptiveAire, led the charge on this project.

Change is always challenging and the fear of the unknown gets the best of many people. The naysayers were anxious about changing the status quo and were uncertain about customer acceptance of this redesign. However, the new design provided CaptiveAire with a huge cost advantage in the market. This was one of the best and most important product decisions ever made in the history of CaptiveAire. Thankfully, most of our competitors failed to follow our lead until much later.

The year before we implemented the metal change, we achieved a thirty-two percent sales gain, with sales of $8.7 million. In 1988, we gained another thirty-three percent increase, with sales of $11.6 million.

In 1988 we also launched a new brand—a basic line of products called "EconAir." The EconAir name had previously been used by a manufacturer's rep and I purchased it from him for our use.

ON THE MOVE AGAIN

Strong sales growth called for increased capacity at all levels, but land costs in our capital city of Raleigh were very high, so it made sense to move out to a neighboring county to the north of us. Our conservative financial management had allowed us to pay off most of our debt, so we were well positioned to buy land and build a third plant to our own specifications.

We decided to create Franklin Park Industrial Center, the first industrial park in the southern part of Franklin County, North Carolina, in 1989. It was initially sixty acres, but it now comprises hundreds of acres. We opened a new 40,000-square-foot plant that allowed us to shorten lead times and boost shipments, and we built several additional buildings and leased them to other manufacturers. We wanted to build hoods on an assembly line at that time but we didn't yet have the product design or knowledge to make the idea feasible. We were able to establish a linear production process beyond the welding booths, which was a start.

In October of 1991, we built a second facility in the park for CaptiveAire and transferred some of our operations to it, including the corporate office. In 1992 we built a new CaptiveAire plant in the park and took over operations of a third facility, which had been rented to another manufacturer. We had 150 employees, and we were continuing to hire. Outside of CaptiveAire's facilities, the industrial park attracted many businesses and entrepreneurs. Today, southern Franklin County is a growing business hub, with shopping centers and thousands of jobs.

In just over ten years, the fledgling fire system installation company, Atlantic Fire Systems, Inc., had morphed into CaptiveAire, a national manufacturer of innovative custom commercial kitchen ventilation systems. We were now poised for rapid future growth, but many challenges remained ahead.

"Entrepreneurial profit is the expression of the value of what the entrepreneur contributes to production."

JOSEPH SCHUMPETER

CHAPTER FOUR

EXPANDING AND EVOLVING 1989–PRESENT

At CaptiveAire we adopted the tradition of most entrepreneurial companies and expanded from organic growth. There were, however, a few exceptions, including a small number of strategic acquisitions in order to gain new technologies.

For example, a company called Aqua-Matic, in Reno, Nevada, had a technology for water-wash hoods, which used spray nozzles to clean the area behind the filters, as well as a unique product called a utility distribution system (UDS) that provided power, gas, and water hook-ups to the cooking equipment. Despite Aqua-Matic's well-known name in the industry, by 1989 the business was struggling and the owner decided to close it. We were able to reach an agreement to purchase the trade name, products, and engineering, and we transferred manufacturing to our North Carolina plant.

My father handled the entire transition including the recruitment of one of Aqua-Matic's technicians, who had excellent product and manufacturing knowledge. The newly acquired technologies afforded us the opportunity to gain new users and market share in the high-end food-service market. The water-wash hoods were eventually transformed into self-cleaning hoods in 2007, but the early technology was important to our engineering and sales teams. The UDS is still a significant part of our product line.

STEADY GROWTH

CaptiveAire's growth continued, with sales reaching $25 million in 1992. It took two years longer than my original projection, but this confirmed my belief that it is better to establish very high goals.

Establishing high expectations was a proven strategy from then on, so without hesitation I immediately set a new five-year sales goal of $50 million by 1997. I must admit that this was probably an outrageous idea, but the goal was achieved as planned, exactly five years later. Our sales continued to climb, as did our profits. I did not know it at the time but this was the beginning of CaptiveAire as an emerging growth company.

Continuous growth is the goal of most entrepreneurial companies, but it is difficult to achieve. My formula is to explore every potential avenue for the growth of product, people, ideas, and methods, and to make the boldest choices possible. Our focus on ventilation has not changed, but our approach has always been dynamic.

Our manufacturing processes have evolved over the years, scaling up to meet the requirements of our growth. Sophisticated software systems have been developed, an alert and well-trained group of producers has been established, and an unwavering commitment to quality and short lead times have ensured that production quantities have greatly increased and quality and value have been continually maximized.

In 1997, we realized that to compete in every region of the U.S. we needed to have plants located around the country. Remote management would be difficult at first, but the short lead times and reduced shipping costs due to plant localization were well-worth the risk. We opened our first out-of-state plant in Muskogee, Oklahoma, in part because of the warm welcome we received from then-Governor Frank Keating and the State of Oklahoma. Muskogee was centrally located in the lower midwest and was near one of our fan suppliers, Acme Engineering. We built a new 100,000-square-foot plant, which provided the capacity to double our production.

This proved to be a fortuitous move, opening up new markets and improving our manufacturing processes with new equipment and methods. We could now ship quickly to the other half of the country, with our west coast shipping time dropping from eight days to four. In addition, the higher capacity output allowed us to support our growing sales teams much more efficiently.

A STEP TOWARDS AUTOMATION

In 1997, we took a big step toward the goal of automation by making fans with modular components, thus facilitating efficient production on assembly lines. Initially this was implemented in our Youngsville plant, but after we gained some experience it was adopted in our new Oklahoma plant as well. The process took a long time to develop and by 2001 we needed an improved product design to gain speed on the line. Once achieved however, we gained remarkable efficiency and significant production increases. This began the modern approach of designing product and process congruently to achieve stellar results.

We were still determined to design a hood that could be produced on an assembly line, but it would take another five years to achieve this goal.

EARLY ACQUISITIONS

In 1999, we acquired the make-up air division (including a factory in West Union, Iowa) from Rupp Industries, a Minnesota-based industrial heating business. Rupp invented direct fired make-up air, now the industry standard for dedicated make-up air. At the time, Rupp had an excellent product but had some quality issues and long lead times, so we worked to solve these problems through hundreds of engineering changes over the first year that improved quality in both large and small ways. We reduced lead times at Rupp from twelve weeks to an average of two to four weeks, and we lowered prices by reducing labor and material costs. Users, sales representatives, and employees appreciate a company that is improving in quality and sales.

The entrepreneurial approach of getting things done quickly and correctly generates opportunities for growth. In 2001, we acquired three small companies at once, which was very unusual for us. The first was FloAire, a small manufacturer of exhaust fans in Bensalem, Pennsylvania. Their manufacturing equipment dated to the 1950s and was no longer safe. Their business was suffering, and we needed a fan line, so we aggressively pursued the purchase. As we experienced with Rupp, this type of acquisition was challenging because the company essentially had to be transformed culturally and financially. Every fan component and process at FloAire was re-engineered to make the products robust and the manufacturing process efficient.

The other two acquisitions in 2001 were Muckler Industries, Inc. (also traded under K-tech), and LDI, located in Logansport, Indiana. Both companies were manufacturers of kitchen hoods, and both were failing and had old facilities with antiquated equipment. We did not want to operate in their environments so both plants were shut down before we took over. Through these acquisitions, we gained new users, along with a few new product ideas. Over the years we also acquired various technologies from other companies who were unsuccessful with them, which further advanced our products. We still manage these acquisitions to this day, selling products under CaptiveAire, RuppAir, FloAire and other names. Growing each brand individually helps us to meet the unique needs of each market segment.

REDESIGNS AND REFORMULATIONS

In 2001, we began a product redesign of our air handlers and heaters. We wanted to create a unit that was composed of individual factory-built modules, allowing a user to mix and match to meet their requirements. These modules could then be bolted together and shipped as one unit, resulting in a quick and easy installation and a faster lead time due to standardization. Bill Griffin, who has been our VP of Engineering since 2003, led the project.

Bill is a graduate of mechanical engineering from the University of Maryland. He not only is incredibly skilled but he also out-thinks and out-works most everyone in the company. In 2000, he was our engineer in charge of retesting all direct fired heaters under new stringent ASTM requirements. This project was extensive and required over a year of testing, but Bill handled it with ease. We quickly realized his talent and promoted him into the top ranks of our engineering leadership, despite his young age. After Bill took on the project of redesigning our air handlers, it soon morphed into a total reformulation of all CaptiveAire products. Each of the redesigns focused on improving quality, performance, and cost. Bill and his team's constant drive to improve provided benefits for our customers and our company.

As the modular make-up air product neared completion, we also worked on the air distribution of make-up air. Delivering outside air to a kitchen may sound simple but it had always been a challenge. We finally realized that a simple plenum delivering air close to the hood, vertically and at low velocities was the key. This recognition culminated in a revolutionary product named the Perforated Supply Plenum (PSP) that could deliver eighty percent of the needed make-up air with minimal tempering, which was a major energy savings. The PSP was released in 2002, and by 2005 we added the ability to deliver building air conditioning in the same device.

We proceeded to develop other new technologies such as pollution control systems for exhausting kitchen odors and effluent, energy management systems, factory-built ductwork, filtration, and a new series of indirect heaters and packaged heating and make-up air systems. We also introduced a revolutionary fire suppression system named CORE that operates like a sprinkler system and uses water to suppress grease fires. More details about these innovations are included in Chapter 7.

CHALLENGES FROM COMPETITORS

In 2002, CaptiveAire became the first company in the history of the kitchen ventilation industry to achieve $100 million in sales. In the past, ours was a splintered industry, with numerous small manufacturers and sheet metal shops. One hundred million dollars was a huge achievement, but early in that same year, we received an alarming threat from one of our competitors. The company believed that they could target and gain twenty-five percent of our business. They announced this plan at their annual sales meeting, and the very next day one of my industry associates called and advised me of the challenge.

We never rest on our accomplishments, and we had already prepared a plan to double our sales within five years. This additional challenge only provided us an extra incentive. We were now armed with the knowledge that our major competitor was aggressively targeting our accounts and in some cases trying to recruit our sales personnel. This information fired up our sales teams as we continued to gain momentum in the market.

If you are going to directly challenge a competitor, it is important to have a well thought-out and executed plan. You also can't underestimate how motivational a challenge like that can be. Business and competition are dynamic in nature; you can't successfully engage in either with static people.

To attack the looming opposition, I analyzed our products, sales, marketing, and quality to make sure we were improving rapidly enough to meet our sales target. We began slowly with only an eight percent sales increase in 2003, but we picked up steam, and by 2005, our growth was strong. We focused most of our energy toward executing orders and achieved a twenty percent sales gain, despite the efforts of our competitor. I have always believed in the power of focus and having high aspirations. Our success in 2005 proved once again that the concepts work.

In the mid 2000s we made several more small acquisitions, including Aerolator, Stratovent, Sun Air, and Grease Master. You may recall we purchased our original hoods in 1977 from Grease Master. They had some talented employees and a strong customer base—a welcome addition to our growth. These acquisitions expanded our customer base and brought in some excellent employees.

ASSEMBLY LINE PRODUCTION OF HOODS

In 2002, we decided to design a new hood that could be constructed on an assembly line. Up to that point, hood assembly had been a lengthy and inefficient process. We aimed to improve the system, but this would require radical changes in both assembly and methods. Complete redesigns of the manufacturing system are difficult to achieve but necessary for growth of product quality and the ability to produce at affordable costs.

Bill Griffin was only twenty-five when the project was assigned to him, but he proved that strong engineering skills and perseverance are what it takes to achieve excellence. In 2004, after two years of arduous design, prototyping, and process developing, the new ND-2 hood was ready for production. It included new fastening devices and allowed us to eliminate flaws and quality issues with our former hood model.

CaptiveAire created a revolutionary new hood design, but more importantly, we introduced the first assembly line for commercial kitchen hoods. Our new manufacturing system utilized some of the ideas we had begun developing in 1987, defining the new standard plant design as a linear process. Each step was reduced to manageable tasks and sub-assembly processes were located near the line to allow for a continuous feed of pre-assembled controls, motors, and dampers as needed. All existing (and future) plants now have this linear design with components entering one end of the plant and processing down assembly lines to the shipping area where completed products are immediately loaded onto trucks and shipped throughout the region.

As a modern manufacturer, we employ machine tools and automation whenever possible to achieve low costs and high quality and output. Hydraulic press brakes use the power of hydraulics and the precision of software to bend metal with great accuracy and repeatability. Automated welders are very precise in temperatures, weld beads, and speed. Aluminum spinning machines produce fan parts safely and rapidly. CNC (Computer Numerical Control) automated benders allow parts to be fabricated quickly, safely, and accurately. These machines require skilled operators, raising the cost of payroll, but ultimately saving expenses in the long run.

NATIONWIDE PLANT EXPANSION

In September of 2004, we moved our main plant into a new 72,000-square-foot facility in Youngsville, North Carolina, a short distance away from its previous location. We moved our corporate office back to Raleigh, to our current location on Paragon Park Road. Many of our employees preferred to work and live in the city and the change provided momentum for growth.

We also opened our first international sales office in Toronto in 2005, which services Canada. This office has maintained consistent growth, opening up new territories for business. Most importantly, the Toronto office helped us to develop the capabilities needed for operating in foreign nations, preparing us for future international ventures.

As a result of the need for regional manufacturing to improve shipping times, we opened a plant in Redding, California, in 2006, and another in Bedford, Pennsylvania, in 2009. Redding is located in northern California along the main Route 5, which is a gateway to the Pacific Northwest and Southern California. Bedford is several hours east of Pittsburgh on the Pennsylvania Turnpike and a gateway to the Northeast, Midwest, and Canada.

Choosing plant locations can be challenging. We looked for excellent work forces and strategic locations, and we considered economic factors such as the land available, tax rates, and the state and local environment for businesses. We also looked for rural locations with adequate labor and supporting communities.

Having five plants in operation ensured that we were a regional manufacturer in every important market in the country with fast delivery times. Many manufacturing companies in recent years have opted to outsource their production operations to other countries, in order to save on labor costs. We've found in our industry, because our products are so large, any savings we'd gain overseas or across borders would be lost in expensive shipping rates. Our strategy takes the opposite approach: spreading regional manufacturing plants throughout the U.S., close to the local market. Most of our shipments arrive in one day with much lower shipping costs than our competitors, ultimately resulting in happier customers.

The years between 2004 and 2007 were prosperous with sales gains of eighteen percent, culminating in $211 million in sales in 2007 and exceeding our goal. We immediately set our sights on $300 million, but our momentum was slowed due to the 2008 financial crisis.

Recessions have often been blessings for our company as we take a harder look at our operations and always come out stronger and leaner. The recent financial crisis was no exception, and after the initial scare of September 2008, we continued to find ways to improve. Our goal of $300 million was delayed, but due to the stringent operations that the recession mandated, the performance of our company is now far superior.

Even during times when the economy is slow, we still aggressively continue product innovations. In the early 2000s, we achieved several major product advancements with our fans, grease filter technologies, and electronic controls, setting us up for success once the market picked back up.

The process of growth continued in 2010 with the introduction of CASService, our service division. We promoted Steve Key as our Service Manager and established service regions throughout the nation to provide in-house service techs to end users in the field. While we always strive to ensure that our products are working properly, occasionally things go wrong and our service personnel are needed to repair equipment. This approach is unique to our company, because most manufacturers in the industry are interested only in selling the initial product. At CaptiveAire, we prefer to maintain a lifelong relationship with our users. We have found that having our own service professionals who quickly diagnose problems and repair equipment results in better outcomes and lower costs for our customers. Today, Steve has grown our service department to sixty service regions and we continue to establish additional regions as required.

In 2011 we opened five new sales offices and continued to open as many for each year following. These new offices allowed us to gain market share within existing territories. Many of them set sales records, which helped reinvigorate older legacy offices. Our competitive advantage originating in 1981 has continued over the years as we look to sell to every potential user in America. Our competitors, who typically sell through traditional independent representatives, have fewer options because the best firms may represent another product. CaptiveAire's method is effective because it allows us to create a new sales division anytime and anywhere we see an opportunity.

In 2012, Bill Griffin and his team of engineers opened a new product development center in East Petersburg, Pennsylvania. This facility of over 20,000 square feet contains a full fire burnout area, along with enough room to test all of our products simultaneously. We emphasize lab and field testing to develop and prove ideas. The process can be slow, but it allows us to design products with high utility and value to the user.

Beginning in 2012, we returned to our long-term growth pattern with sales growing at a fifteen percent increase. For the first time in our history, our sales exceeded one quarter billion dollars.

In 2013, we opened our sixth manufacturing plant in Groveland, Florida, a rural town forty minutes west of Orlando. The Groveland factory services Florida (a major market that greatly benefits from a regional manufacturer) as well as Latin America. Originally the Groveland plant was supposed to be a smaller facility, but as sales expanded in the region, we quickly realized we needed to expand operations. We doubled the size of the factory only about a year after it opened.

The early 2000s brought a host of new products to our offering. Factory built single wall and double wall (insulated) grease ductwork was developed to improve the performance and installation of duct. Traditionally, ductwork is built and welded in the field, but is prone to leaks and takes several days to install. Our duct is built in small sections and is tested for leaks in the factory, and requires only a simple installation process of connecting duct pieces together with V-clamps.

CORE, our water based fire suppression system, continued to improve, and was also expanded to be included in our pollution control unit (PCU) as well as in the duct and hood. CORE is extremely reliable, and has never failed us in a fire situation.

In 2013, we developed CASLink, an in-house building management software system. CASLink allows users to have remote access and control of all building equipment, including kitchen equipment, HVAC, and lighting. It collects data 24/7, enabling us to catch any problems very early on, and allowing for post hoc analysis to improve system efficiency. CASLink is an evolving technology and ultimately will help us improve our products to an even greater degree.

2015 introduced the high volume low speed (HVLS) fan, an efficient ventilation solution for large spaces. HVLS fans have been growing in popularity in recent years and are available from a number of companies. We believe ours is superior due to the energy saving tubercle technology incorporated into the fan blade design.

In 2016, we developed SpecBuilder, an online software program that allows engineers to create product specifications on their own, without the assistance of a salesperson. This product is still in beta, but will serve as a beneficial tool for our users as we move into the modern era.

At the beginning of 2017, we launched our most significant product to date. Paragon, a Dedicated Outdoor Air System, or DOAS, is a highly efficient HVAC unit for commercial spaces that allows for precise humidity and temperature control. Paragon utilizes numerous state-of-the-art technologies to provide the best possible system performance and energy savings for the user. It is an important product in our history, but more importantly, it marks the entrance of CaptiveAire into an entirely new market: the HVAC industry. For four decades we have been known for commercial kitchen ventilation, but we are now expanding into a much broader space encompassing the full gamut of commercial and industrial ventilation.

Accompanying the release of Paragon, we also doubled down on efforts to grow our RuppAir brand. RuppAir has traditionally served the industrial ventilation market (rather than kitchen ventilation), and with the release of the DOAS, this provides an entirely new opportunity for RuppAir. We are excited to watch the growth of this segment of our company in the coming years.

Throughout all of our markets, we have an increasing international presence; CaptiveAire is the dominant supplier in Canada and is an emerging supplier in Mexico. Our technologies are being adopted in places such as Colombia, Central America, and the Caribbean.

A FAMILY BUSINESS

From the beginning, CaptiveAire has always been a family company. In addition to the enormous contributions made by my father and siblings, we employ several cousins and relatives who work in areas including accounting, IT, sales, and plant management.

My children Julie and Randy have proved to be enormous assets to the company. Julie oversees the design and aesthetics of our large network of private and charter Pre-K - 12 schools (you'll learn more about the Luddy Schools in Chapter 10). Her husband, Michael Roach, serves as the development and facilities manager of all future and current school campuses. He handles the entire construction process of building a new campus, from initial land acquisition to opening day. His efforts have been extremely helpful and have significantly expedited the growth of our schools.

Randy is a prime mover at CaptiveAire and has helped us transition our company to the modern era. He assists in general operations, oversees our IT/software development department, manages our Ventilation Direct brand, and contributes to our marketing and branding strategy. I like to joke that Randy is never satisfied and can always give me a list of things I'm doing wrong and should do better. I guess my constant preaching of continuous improvement was well received.

In 2004 I remarried. My wife Maria is an English teacher and after we married she taught high school grammar at one of our schools. She frequently helps me edit my business and economic writings, and she is a daily source of support and ideas.

A family business can be difficult for all but it also unites the family in many ways. The challenge is to keep everyone focused on the goals and outcomes and keep in mind what Dr. Peterson taught us: "None of us get it all right all the time." I am blessed to have had the backing of my family members at every juncture and with every new undertaking. I could not have had the success I've had without their constant encouragement and stellar contributions.

A LIFETIME OF DECISIONS

Over the past forty-plus years, CaptiveAire has transitioned from very humble beginnings as a local systems installer to an emerging technology company serving users in North, Central, and South America. We began in 1976 with only $1,300 capital and a focus on redefining simple processes. Today we are the leader of our industry with sales exceeding $450 million. With the introduction of the Dedicated Outdoor Air System, we are forging into the HVAC market, opening scores of new opportunities for the future of CaptiveAire. For the past twenty years we have doubled sales every five years, and we expect to maintain this pace as we move into the future.

It is important to emphasize the extraordinary effort necessary to achieve lofty goals in an entrepreneurial venture. Hard work must be combined with innovative thinking skills and prudent judgment. The relentless pursuit of truth, quality, and up-to-date technologies should be paired with great execution. In the end, although some business decisions are more critical than others, the success or failure of a business is based on the accumulation of all decisions made over many years.

In the remaining chapters, I will discuss concepts related to the most important aspects of entrepreneurial management and the way we handle business at CaptiveAire, culled from my many years of experience. I learned most of these lessons the hard way, or through extensive research and gleaning of knowledge from mentors. I hope that you, the reader, find these approaches helpful, but ultimately each entrepreneur must develop his or her own style and approach.

PHOTOGRAPHS

THE LUDDY FAMILY C. 1961. TOP ROW, LEFT TO RIGHT: MIKE, STEVE, JOAN, DAVID, JEANIE. BOTTOM ROW, LEFT TO RIGHT: ELAINE, BILL (MY FATHER), BILL (MY BROTHER), ME (BOB), ANGIE (MY MOTHER).

A FRIEND AND I VISITING MY PARENTS' HOUSE IN WILLOW GROVE, PA, SHORTLY AFTER I JOINED THE ARMY, C. 1968.

JULIE, RANDY, AND ME C. 1986 AT MY PARENTS' HOUSE.

JULIE AND RANDY VACATIONING WITH MY PARENTS IN
WRIGHTSVILLE BEACH C. 1989. NOTE RANDY'S POSITRAK T-SHIRT.

GEORGE GENDRON, EDITOR IN CHIEF OF *INC.* MAGAZINE, CONGRATULATING
CAPTIVEAIRE ON BEING NAMED #43 IN THE 1986 *INC.* 500. WE CONTINUED TO
WIN THIS AWARD FOR MANY YEARS AFTER.

TWO FORMER EMPLOYEES AND ME AT THE 1987 ASHRAE
TRADE SHOW IN NEW YORK CITY.

ATTENDING A TRADE SHOW, C. 1988.

JUDY NUNNENKAMP AND TWO FORMER
CAPTIVEAIRE EMPLOYEES IN 1988.

BILL FRANCIS, A COLLEAGUE, AND ME AT AN EVENT IN 1993.

MY FATHER AND I READING ONE AFTERNOON, C. 1993.
WE SHARED A PASSION FOR CONTINUOUS LEARNING.

THE RIBBON CUTTING CEREMONY FOR OUR MUSKOGEE, OK PLANT IN 1997.

DR. PETERSON AND ME, C. 1998. THE THEORIST AND THE ENTREPRENEUR.

MY WIFE, MARIA, AND I VACATIONING IN SALZBURG, AUSTRIA IN 2010.

THE LAST PHOTO OF DR. PETERSON AND ME, TAKEN IN 2011,
THE YEAR BEFORE HE PASSED AWAY.

LEFT TO RIGHT: MY SISTER JEANIE, HER HUSBAND HARRY SILLETTI,
MY MOTHER ANGIE, MY BROTHER STEVE, C. 2012.

LEFT TO RIGHT: MY BROTHER DAVE, ME, MY SISTER ELAINE, MY BROTHER MIKE,
AND MY BROTHER STEVE IN 2012.

BILL GRIFFIN AND ME AT OUR CORPORATE OFFICE IN 2015.

OUR RESEARCH AND DEVELOPMENT LAB IN LANCASTER, PA.

THE CONTROL BOARD FOR OUR CORE FIRE SUPPRESSION SYSTEM.

A STATE-OF-THE-ART HOOD SYSTEM IN A CAPTIVEAIRE DISPLAY CENTER.

FRANKLIN ACADEMY, THE CHARTER SCHOOL I FOUNDED IN 1997.

ST. THOMAS MORE ACADEMY, THE PRIVATE CATHOLIC HIGH SCHOOL
I FOUNDED IN 2001.

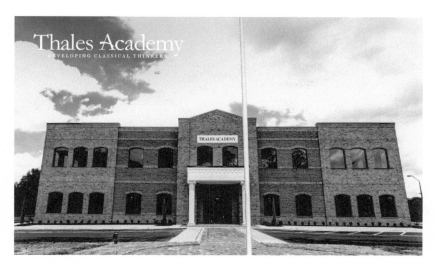

THALES ACADEMY, THE CHAIN OF PRIVATE SCHOOLS I FOUNDED IN 2007.
PICTURED IS A PRE-K-5 CAMPUS.

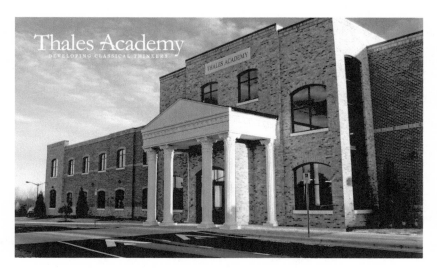

THALES ACADEMY, THE CHAIN OF PRIVATE SCHOOLS I FOUNDED IN 2007.
PICTURED IS A JH/HS CAMPUS.

PART TWO

ENTREPRENEURIAL MANAGEMENT

"Whereas it is always a joy to praise those deserving praise, it should be a source of regret to have to criticize others, even when their error is likely to poison other people."

DR. ALICE VON HILDEBRAND

CHAPTER FIVE

MENTORING

The process of entrepreneurial management requires a continuous flow of new information, discussions, challenges, experience, and review. It is important to mine every possible source of wisdom. Perhaps the best instruction is taken from those who have been there and have become the masters in their fields. As I like to say, "Learn from the masters."

Every day we meet people who have more experience or knowledge than we do, and each is a potential mentor. These mentors can help us gain insights much more quickly than we can on our own. Most of the best opportunities in life are within our range of observation, but we must be alert to perceive them and respond with superior insight by asking questions and seeking advice. We can then allow our mentors' influence to take effect and add to our composite of knowledge and wisdom. Unfortunately, chances to learn from others are easily missed, so we must refine our ability to stay alert and recognize significant moments when they occur. You never know when a piece of advice may be useful.

EARLY MENTORS

I have benefitted enormously from interactions with mentors, especially my parents. My siblings and I received a solid foundation; our parents instilled in us the belief that every person can make a difference in the world. They supported and encouraged us in all of our efforts, and their influence on us has been incredibly beneficial and long lasting.

In high school I had two important mentors: Dr. Galen Bayer, at the pharmacy in Harrisburg, and Dr. Tilman Foust, the neighbor who taught me about investments. The encouragement of both was critical to my early life.

In college I was able to find a job in another local pharmacy in Philadelphia working for Dr. Mark Cohen, who turned out to be my next important mentor. He instilled solid values and a good moral philosophy, along with common sense business skills I have used throughout my life. At that time I was considering becoming a lawyer, but he told me, "No, you are not. You're going to be an entrepreneur." He had the right vision for my personal interests before I was even aware of them myself.

When I graduated from college and my military deferment expired, it was necessary to sell the fiberglass business, Uni-form Fiberglass, that I had founded with a partner. Fortunately we were able to sell it to the owner of another manufacturer, Crouse and Company, where I continued to work during my final months before entering the Army.

Jim Crouse was the founder and CEO, and I reported directly to him. He was a great teacher and thinker and he took a personal interest in my career. Through his influence, I learned how an effective entrepreneur thinks and executes. Mr. Crouse began as a heating and ventilation contractor and eventually became a prime contractor building nuclear power plants. Jim was known as a shrewd trader, because he knew how to drive a hard bargain. I only worked for him for a short time, but the lessons he taught me were long-lasting.

Golden Corral, which now has over 200 locations, is a major customer of CaptiveAire. Co-founders James Maynard and Bill Carl were vital mentors for me, particularly in the early days of my company. The opportunity to observe their fast-growing operation and learn about entrepreneurial business from them was invaluable. Mr. Maynard always stressed the importance of every person's success and the value of incentives, making us all winners.

LEARNING FROM THE MASTERS

The people who influence us the most are not always the ones with whom we spend the most time. In 1991, I had the good fortune to spend a day with the then president of Nucor Steel, the late Ken Iverson.

The recipient of the Robert P. Stupp Award for Leadership Excellence by the American Institute of Steel Construction, Ken was voted the best steel executive in the world. During a time when the American steel industry in general was struggling to remain profitable (1965-1998), Ken transformed his company from a small, unprofitable conglomerate into a large, highly successful steel company.

He began the steel manufacturing at Nucor soon after he was appointed CEO, and due to his commitment to meet very high levels of efficiency and productivity, built it into the largest steel maker in the U.S. He did so by balancing a number of factors including an investment strategy, technology, marketing, and excellent management.

One of the most important concepts I learned from Ken was his productive incentive system—the creation of incentives for all employees, which ensures that everyone has a vested interest in corporate profits. Done correctly, employees become just as interested in profits as shareholders. We have implemented this system at CaptiveAire for over twenty-five years now and it has been a resounding success and a huge driver in employee productivity. Manufacturing employees receive monthly bonuses from their plant's profits, salespeople from their respective regions, and administrative employees from overall results.

All bonuses are also performance related, and thus vary on an individual basis depending on personal effort. The monthly bonus program is greatly appreciated by our employees and helps all to understand the real link between sales and production and profitability. In shorter months with fewer production days, bonuses decrease, and vice versa. It's a simple economic concept that really helps employees see the big picture when it affects personal pay. It also serves as a great motivational tool when performance is lacking or deserves extra appreciation.

Ken also taught me about what I term "radical decentralization of operations," which we quickly adopted (explained in detail in the next chapter). Nucor, under Iverson, had only eighteen central office employees for a multibillion dollar corporation, which was in line with his passion for efficiency. Ken perfected decentralization and developed the most efficient steel company in America. He understood value creation, and he knew the importance of jobs to rural communities. Ken provided good-paying jobs for those who met the company's requirements. Most Nucor employees make more than union employees because they are more productive.

It is imperative to learn from the masters. Mentors such as Ken Iverson provide wisdom that is not easily gleaned from books—they fill in the details that support and make their ideas work realistically. CaptiveAire grew organically, and while we had a lot of business experience in our people, we often didn't have some of the higher-level innovative corporate ideas that successful companies develop. That changed with Mr. Iverson's insight.

I will be forever grateful to Mr. Iverson for his time and advice. I only had one afternoon to learn from him when he was a speaker at Meredith College at a leadership program, but the lessons he taught have stayed with me and influenced our company for decades.

MENTORS AS FRIENDS

In 1991, I discovered another vital mentor when I was asked to speak at a business and leadership seminar for the Adam Smith Club at Campbell University in North Carolina. While there, I met Dr. Peterson, to whom this book is dedicated. At that time he was the Lundy Chair of Economics and Business Philosophy at the school. Prior to that, he was a tenured professor at New York University and other schools, the chief economist for U. S. Steel, and a writer for many prestigious publications including *The Wall Street Journal,* where he had a weekly column for 20 years. Later he wrote for publishers and educational institutions including the Mises Institute and the Foundation for Economic Education (FEE).

Dr. Peterson studied under Ludwig von Mises at New York University. Mises was the leading Austrian School economist of the 20th century and advocated free market principles. He completely changed Dr. Peterson's thinking about economics. Over the course of the next twenty years, Dr. Peterson, a notable economist and teacher in his own right, taught me much of what he had learned from Mises and other economists. We became close friends and it was a sad day when he departed from this life.

My chance meeting with him illustrates an important point: I was taking some time out to speak to students but ended up gaining a wealth of knowledge from my new mentor.

Of course, not every mentor in my life was a high level theorist. Some mentors were down-to-earth people who focused on their own backyards, and who inspired me to better myself in areas outside of business. Harry Eberly is a retired businessman and chemical engineer who devoted his time to improving society. He facilitates every project by bringing both great ideas and resources to the table. He's a natural mentor who has developed contacts in business, educational, and civic arenas over many years.

Harry's office was beside mine in Highwood's Office Park in 1990. We met when he introduced himself and asked for some help on a playground project sponsored by the Raleigh Chamber of Commerce. We have since worked together on various civic and governmental projects for over twenty-five years. His wisdom, integrity, and knowledge have made me a better person. Sometimes we forget how many great people live in this world; Harry is one of the best.

HISTORICAL FIGURES

Several famous entrepreneurs have also profoundly affected my life, even though their lives ended long before I was born. I enjoy reading biographies of people who have been successful in different arenas, and try to apply what I learn to my own endeavors.

The Wright brothers are two of my favorite entrepreneurs because they encompassed so many great attributes, such as self-reliance and independence. They used a scientific approach but they had the wisdom to sort out the correct answers and jettison incorrect conventional ideas. They embraced the entrepreneurial approach to creating new concepts and changing the world, they were lifetime learners, and they valued self-teaching. Although neither of the brothers graduated from high school, they worked extensively to educate themselves, and as a result, each possessed learning equal to a four-year degree.

I have learned much from Ben Franklin as well. Most consider him a Renaissance man if ever there was one. He was a printer, author, philanthropist, inventor, statesman, diplomat, and scientist. He was also a Member of Congress—the Continental Congress—that laid the groundwork for American independence. Along with serving as the founding member of the Library Company of Philadelphia, Franklin contributed to establishing a volunteer fire department and police service. Throughout his numerous accomplishments, Ben Franklin understood the importance of a solid education. By establishing a library in Philadelphia, he provided citizens with an opportunity to learn and develop new knowledge and skills.

In many ways, Ben Franklin inspired my own love for learning and desire to help educate others. The primary lesson I learned from Mr. Franklin is to never stop experimenting and growing as a person, as he did until he died at age eighty-four.

Much has been written about Steve Jobs, but for good reason. He was the most important entrepreneur and innovator of my lifetime. His goal was simple but profound, as he wished only "to change the world." Steve taught all of us to reach for the unthinkable and then make it a reality. This process essentially defines the pinnacle of entrepreneurship.

Each and every one of these mentors helped me challenge our team to utilize the philosophies of constant critique and daily improvement. Aiming for perfection is second nature to the successful entrepreneur. The example of a relentless desire for excellence by all of my mentors has played a huge role in the success of CaptiveAire. To my many mentors, thank you for patiently sharing your time and knowledge. I am immensely grateful for your wisdom.

MENTORING OTHERS

In 1986 I was asked to be the principal speaker at North Carolina State University for an organization called SCORE (Service Corps of Retired Executives), a mentoring institution that helps small businesses get off the ground and achieve their goals through education and business counseling. I continued working with the group for about a dozen years. It was a win-win because I was able to pass on some of what I'd learned as well as meet the other SCORE volunteers and learn from their experiences.

I have been fortunate to serve as a mentor for many of my employees as well. Many former CaptiveAire team members, having learned the skills of entrepreneurism, have departed to begin new businesses of their own. One of our prime subcontractors, Robbie Tilley, was an excellent welder and layout mechanic during his fifteen-year tenure at CaptiveAire. Robbie now makes large quantities of sheet metal components using these and other capabilities he learned at CaptiveAire. Another, Brandon Wellington, was an engineer for us before he decided to leave CaptiveAire to start his own commercial kitchen ventilation service venture. We still continue to work with his company today.

In 1990, we hired Bill Bland as one of our product designers, and later he was promoted to plant manager of Aqua-Matic in 1992. He advanced quickly and was one of our best employees. In 1993, I asked him to supervise the renovation of our old plant at Bramer Drive in Raleigh, and thereafter he handled all of our construction. He did a superb job and eventually founded a division constructing metal buildings for industry, which we called "Cade, Inc."

One of the buildings we built was St. Catherine of Siena Catholic Church in Wake Forest, North Carolina. (I am a member of the parish, and they were growing and desperate for a new church but had limited funds.) After three years, I sold Cade, Inc. to Bill and he has done very well over the past fifteen-plus years. Cade has handled many of our new building construction projects for both our offices and schools. According to Bill, both the experience and business knowledge he gained at CaptiveAire were an important part of his later success.

Two former employees who managed our Cincinnati office, Olaf Zwickau and Joe Hertenstein, also decided to become entrepreneurs in their own right. They started a business called Air Solutions, which offered CaptiveAire products but added installation and test and balance services. Later Olaf split from Joe and opened his own branch of Air Solutions in New Hampshire. He recently contacted me to say that, after struggling hard to make his company work, he is doing very well. Today, after ten-plus years in business, he has a multimillion dollar company with its own building and several employees. He credits his days selling CaptiveAire products as a mentoring time for him. One key concept he learned is that all businesses involve great adversity and struggles, so he was not surprised when he faced them himself.

David Duke was a former layout technician but now runs his own fabrication business. He can make any custom product from metal, including fences, cabinets and a range of sheet-metal products.

I am immensely proud of these former employees and support their goal of self-employment. These outcomes illustrate the importance of the process of entrepreneurial growth and its impact on the economy, job creation, and the introduction of new technologies in the marketplace.

In recent years, I have also had the great joy of mentoring a number of students, including those enrolled at our schools, summer interns at CaptiveAire, and students participating in groups I am involved in, such as the Calvin Coolidge Presidential Foundation. In my later years, I have found that it is extremely fulfilling to impart my knowledge to others, especially young individuals. It gives me hope to know that a new generation is inspired to contribute and change the world in its own ways.

KEY TAKEAWAYS:

- Learn from the masters.

- You can learn something from every person you meet.

- Entrepreneurial management requires a continuous flow of new information and ideas.

- Stay alert and recognize potential mentors when they cross your path. Learn as much as you can from them, whether you interact with them for three hours or three years. Ask questions to gain a full understanding.

- Learn from historical or celebrity mentors as well as personal ones.

- Share your knowledge and mentor others when given the opportunity.

"Management is doing things right;
leadership is doing the right things."

PETER DRUCKER

CHAPTER SIX

LEADERSHIP

Entrepreneurs think and act differently than other people, which is why they often achieve extraordinary success. The intellectual and physical energy they bring to a project separates them from the crowd. They are great risk managers, who relish change and have visions far beyond conventional wisdom.

"Entrepreneurial talent cannot be purchased in the market place," said Ludwig von Mises. "[Entrepreneurs] are often dissatisfied with the way things are done. No matter how good things are, the entrepreneur thinks they can and should be better."

These traits that an entrepreneur brings to an organization can be extremely valuable, but only when utilized properly. Leadership must be understood and practiced, for it stands as the cornerstone of any company. The leader sets the vision, breaks it down into goals, prioritizes the objectives, and assigns responsibility in order to ensure that the vision is achieved. Managers and team leads encourage employees in the implementation of the goal. True leadership blended with entrepreneurial talents facilitates excellence through strong customer relationships, thinking beyond current technologies, and constantly updating and executing a well thought out growth plan.

EXECUTION

Execution is the most difficult part of management. In his book *Execution: The Discipline of Getting Things Done,* Larry Bossidy indicates that most failures result from poor execution, not incompetence. The goals and the methods for achievement should be reiterated frequently. Every leader should harness the best talent available and empower his or her team every day to achieve major challenges.

Some companies stress process but I stress execution as our highest priority. All success must be measured in terms of outcome—what was actually accomplished. Processes may support and contribute to a rapid response and outcome, but they cannot be the goal themselves. Too often, companies develop lengthy rule books for handling situations. They claim, "Well we followed the process!" But they forget the end goal because all attention is on process alone. It doesn't matter how long we've spent developing new methods and procedures, if in the end, they don't work. Everything must be measured in terms of real outcome.

Service is an important component of effective execution; the task must be performed efficiently and delivered with excellent customer service. I always ask, "How quickly can a task be completed, and when will it be ready?" If a customer calls, our priority is to serve in real time, not at our convenience. Many businesses fail this challenge because process impedes service.

Mises explains the execution process in this way: "Action is preceded by thinking. Thinking is to deliberate beforehand over future action and to reflect afterward upon past action. Thinking and acting are inseparable." The chart below describes this process. First, you must develop your thinking skills, which lead to good ideas, which then must be executed and put into action. This is a daily process that improves and advances over time, as you hone your skills and build your knowledge.

THE DAILY EXECUTION PROCESS

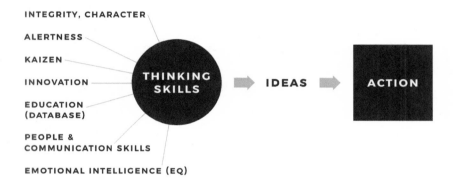

INTEGRITY, CHARACTER

ALERTNESS

KAIZEN

INNOVATION

EDUCATION
(DATABASE)

PEOPLE &
COMMUNICATION SKILLS

EMOTIONAL INTELLIGENCE (EQ)

THINKING SKILLS → IDEAS → ACTION

An entrepreneur must be anticipating the future at all times and executing the best ideas to achieve growth. A plan is nothing but a good intention unless it is executed. This requires a fanatical commitment by leaders who consistently challenge themselves, their companies, and accepted norms.

It is very important to steer one's company away from pitfalls and allow it to successfully navigate and develop competitive advantages. As a leader, you must be concerned about many things, some of which may never happen. Many negative outcomes can be avoided through good thinking and execution.

DECISION MAKING

Thinking and acting quickly are critical skills imperative to an entrepreneur's leadership. Successful entrepreneurs must make consistently good decisions based on the knowledge and information available at the time, along with a healthy dose of informed intuition. Bureaucrats frequently demand additional information but entrepreneurs have no such luxury. This is a complex process, but if decisions are delayed, opportunities may be lost. Many leaders prefer to have a preponderance of information before deciding, but as Ken Iverson taught me, "at least thirty percent of the decisions made by the most experienced executives could be improved." Every venture is a risk; there is never a sure thing.

The marketplace, like the world, is as we find it. The way we react to it makes all the difference. The author of *Chicken Soup for the Soul,* Jack Canfield, summed it up this way: "Event + Response = Outcome." We can't control many events, but we can control our responses and the decisions we make with regards to them, and thus we can change the outcome. Leadership requires us to meet the challenges at hand and the marketplace forces us to see things as they are, not as we would wish them to be. Leaders must accept and overcome these daily obstacles in order to survive and prosper.

Successful entrepreneurs must carefully evaluate every decision after the fact and review failed opportunities to improve future judgment. If we misread the requirements of our users, failure often follows. This review does not necessarily lead to new technologies, innovations, or approaches, but frequently provides more insight into our weaknesses and how to best manage the business.

LEAN, FLAT MANAGEMENT STRUCTURE

We have a unique leadership style at CaptiveAire that allows for enough structure to avoid chaos, but is fluid enough to support rapid change and lightning-fast decisions.

About twenty years ago, we decentralized as a result of the lessons that I had learned from Ken Iverson (described in Chapter 5). It was a challenge, but it refocused us on customer service rather than on process. We shifted the focus from the corporate office to the regional field offices. They communicate directly with the plants.

Decentralizing ensured that sales and technical people were brought together on a localized basis in order to fully serve customers, eliminating the need for a large and unproductive central office. Today, out of our approximately 1,200 employees in the company, only eighty or so work out of our headquarters. These corporate office employees are primarily engaged in information technology, finance and accounting, and human resources.

A decentralized organization works because centralization often breeds bureaucracy and retards processes. The "principle of subsidiarity" means that all decisions are made at the lowest level possible and quickly. I could cite many examples but here are a few:

- Each sales team controls application engineering, pricing, and customer service. Quality and application design standards, automatically generated CAD drawings, and our point-of-sale software support our sales operations.

- Credit and collection personnel make important decisions every hour but are guided by our customer-centered philosophy, common sense, and good business judgment. It can be a big challenge to collect money and keep customers happy but they execute almost flawless collection for 99.80 percent of all accounts receivable.

- Quality control engineers must make their own judgments determining whether products meet standards and work in harmony with the pace and stresses of production.

- Software developers write code, transforming complex products into workable selection software for our users. This process is worked out with the users and engineers, not senior management.

Today we function much more like a united group of small enterprises including manufacturing, sales, service, product development, finance, and administration, than like a large company. What we have found is that complex management structures impede decision-making and drive customers to competitors, so our flat management structure saves costs and increases performance.

Heavy-handed managers are not welcome in modern business and certainly not in our company. Each individual requires skill to manage his or her tasks, and deserves recognition and trust based on performance. To that end we seek self-reliant and tenacious individuals with consistent, flexible attitudes. We are constantly changing as a result of continuous improvement and this creates challenges for everyone. Only those who thrive on change and innovation reach the ranks of our highest professionals.

Autonomy is a reward stemming from our "Empowered Employee" philosophy. Those who prove to be highly reliable are not closely managed, and they have the freedom to create and grow without being stifled by too many rules. The only rule we consistently maintain is that employees must do their jobs at a level of excellence. Any regulation beyond this can quickly lead to frustrated personnel and subsequent poor performance, so we keep all rulemaking to a minimum. Employees who prove their skills are easily considered "empowered," and they naturally meet corporate goals of growth, quality, and customer service with integrity.

A result of our "Empowered Employee" philosophy is that team members are encouraged to change current processes and methods if needed. Those who identify obstacles and challenges and provide beneficial solutions are praised and rewarded, regardless of tenure or position. Our employees are solution providers who figure out how to improve long-term growth at all levels. In all that we do, we disdain conventionality and find a way to win.

Eliminating bureaucracy and trusting astute leadership at all levels allows the company to focus on what is most important: the creation of value and the servicing of the user's requirements. Pride and power are disregarded, allowing cooperative teamwork to earn the greatest gains in the end.

BUILDING A WINNING CULTURE

Although sometimes overlooked, corporate culture often determines the overall direction of a company's motion; it is important to make sure that the majority of your team is moving toward your goals. The entrepreneur and other main drivers must set the example and live by it consistently in order to show employees how things are best performed. For example, I am a huge proponent of being on time for work. In order to set a positive example, I arrive an hour before my team each morning, and usually stay later than most employees. I never ask my employees to work harder than I do, but my behavior serves as a daily reminder and inspiration to reach higher. The culture should flow from the top down, spreading attitudes, ideals, and key objectives to every level of the team.

Employees are sometimes dubious about lofty goals and may assume that goals cannot be met, so they must continually be encouraged to find new ways to win. They must embrace creativity, curiosity, and constructive conflict with speed, agility, and adaptation, but these traits are only obtainable if the leader personally reflects and communicates all of these values first.

A business should also maintain a positive attitude to ease the difficulties of tackling major projects. Every success opens the opportunity for new growth and provides a team with the confidence and energy required for the next big undertaking. The joy of work—the excitement of making a sale, designing a new product, coding software, serving users—is intrinsic if the environment is positive.

UNITING A TEAM

Entrepreneurial founders are creative and dynamic drivers, but they require the assistance of those who possess complementary skills to effectively serve their customers. Entrepreneurs may like to think they're experts at everything, but that's not possible. They require the counsel and balance specialists can contribute, and although the proper cooperation among these specialists is difficult, it is critical to achieve sustainable success. The entrepreneur aids in this process, as he or she serves as the binding agent for all of the numerous aspects of a company.

Every good team starts with high-caliber individuals. Maury Klein stated in his book *The Change Makers,* "All human achievement is based on the individual. Working within teams is important, but achievement is singularly individual." This quote is illustrative of the requirements for leadership within a team and stresses the importance of individual contribution. You must develop and support the individuals of your team and encourage them to achieve their individual best.

During this process, leaders must recognize and eliminate employees who do not share the company vision or who lack the values or talents needed to push the company toward success. We hope that everyone will be in agreement in order to accomplish common objectives, but at times, this is not the case, so it is necessary to remove the "blockers," or individuals who do not share our goals. Although this is a difficult task, it is required if you wish to attain peak performance and ultimate happiness of both parties. People who appreciate your intentions are much easier to work with, and are generally happier than those who feel as though they are forced to conform.

Once a strong group of individuals has been cultivated, you must encourage a spirit of cooperative teamwork to reach a success greater than the individual parts. Honest and candid dialogue must be fostered among employees, and all contributing members should be heard, regardless of tenure or experience, before finalizing decisions. This allows junior members of the team to contribute and very often promotes positive and innovative change.

It can be difficult to gather one cooperative group because everyone involved has different values and needs. Each employee sees the business through his or her own lens, and sometimes these perspectives are at odds. For example, the sales representatives want easy credit for their customers, while the finance team wants rigid credit policies to ensure collection of accounts receivable. Very strong leadership is often necessary to avoid turf wars and conflicts of values. The leader must be sensitive and only jump in when required. The judgment of the leader must be under constant refinement as the challenges are formidable and unrelenting.

At CaptiveAire, we constantly stress cooperation and try to drive out ineffective bureaucracy so that the processes serve the users rather than requiring the users to serve the process. If the process stifles service, customers will move to more efficient providers. Many businesses miss this important point, to their detriment.

RETAINING EMPLOYEES

Retaining talented employees is imperative to growth and as a result we have many programs in place to create a productive and cooperative environment. We provide catered lunches in our factories on a monthly basis and in our corporate office on a weekly basis. We send out monthly recognitions of longevity for tenure of 3, 5, 10, 15, 20, 25 and 30 years of service; at year-end these employees receive plaques and a financial reward. We build aesthetically pleasing offices for our employees, outfitting spaces with modern design and generous amenities.

Each employee is given beyond adequate technological resources. In the theme of pursuing excellence, we believe in the superiority of Apple products in most routine technical applications. All office employees are provided with a combination of iMacs, MacBooks, iPads, additional monitors, and other accessories according to the job requirements of each position. Our engineering and IT personnel are provided with all of the testing and development equipment that they need to carry out their tasks. We do not skimp on resources, because we know that the best possible outcomes will result when our team has everything they need to complete their tasks.

We make it a point to recognize employees for their contributions whenever warranted, whether via email, on the phone, or during a company webinar. When announcing a new feature or development, we take a few seconds to recognize and thank the individual(s) who contributed to it. This is a small and simple gesture but goes a long way in helping employees feel appreciated for their work.

Perhaps one of the most valued benefits that our team enjoys is our low drama environment and avoidance of micromanagement. Many employees consider the working environment at CaptiveAire to be a relief after working for other companies, despite our high demands and performance expectations.

These are all small details, but by actively demonstrating that we respect and appreciate our employees, all of our team members feel more satisfied and welcomed into our mission. This fosters a greater spirit of productivity among our team, and allows us to have the opportunity to show that we care.

STREAMLINED COMMUNICATION SYSTEMS

At CaptiveAire, we don't have regularly scheduled meetings, and even impromptu meetings are rare. Meetings remove your most productive talent from the playing field, which is in conflict with a strong customer focus. They tend to waste large amounts of time and most can be avoided.

The only meetings we have are brief strategy and product development sessions. When necessary, individual meetings are normally short and highly productive. Our last general sales meeting was held in 2007. We have had some regional sales meetings for product and innovation rollouts, but they usually last just one day and are held every other year on average. The last thing a customer wants to hear is, "Our salesperson is in an important sales meeting and will contact you next week." Even during meetings, our personnel respond to priority emails.

We consider phone calls and voicemail to be outdated processes for many reasons; however, a small number of phone calls can be useful to sort out fine details. In our offices, voicemails are converted to emails and therefore best avoided. We prefer to communicate in most situations through emailing, which provides a clear record and the fastest possible response. Emails are written as informal and concise as possible, to further improve efficiency. Quick questions are often handled through instant messaging, even if both correspondents are located in the same building. Efficiency is maximized in all communications, whenever possible.

Our primary teaching tool is the webinar. One of the drawbacks of a decentralized team is the difficulty of communicating information to the entire team at once. Webinars allow us to maintain unity of purpose and stay connected with employees across the country.

Each month we have webinars with our quality and production managers, usually only lasting about twenty minutes. We provide the status on important quality, procurement, safety, sales, and production goals. We also host technical webinars for all sales personnel to provide in-depth training on new products and technologies.

About once per month we have a webinar for all personnel. I provide an update on management philosophy, status on sales and production, kudos for important accomplishments, and an emphasis on our goals. Bill Griffin, our VP of Engineering, provides information on engineering changes, new products, and application engineering.

Every other month, we have a webinar focusing on a selected book or reading to improve personal development. We call this series "Bob's Book Review," and use it as an opportunity to learn from others in a variety of fields. It also allows me to mentor our team on a more personal and less business-focused level. Employees enjoy the opportunity to broaden their knowledge and ultimately, it helps improve performance across the company overall.

These webinars, which typically average thirty minutes, allow every CaptiveAire team member to be informed firsthand about how the company is doing and where we are headed. Anyone on the call can ask questions by email. If an individual is unable to attend a webinar, it is recorded for future use and is available online.

Throughout all communication methods, employees are encouraged to challenge ideas presented, which improves the process. The group ferrets out issues we may have failed to recognize, and these are always carefully reviewed. It is the responsibility of leadership to understand and find the best possible solutions to challenging problems.

CONTINUOUS IMPROVEMENT

Continuous improvement is a crucial standard at CaptiveAire, and over time, most team members come to realize how critically important this concept is to growth. Many years ago, I discovered the Japanese concept of "Kaizen," which is a formal process of improvement. It was developed from the war-torn environment in Japan following World War II, and many companies have since adapted it as a highly effective method of management.

Japanese industry, especially heavy industry, was in shambles due to the atomic bombings at the end of World War II. The process of rebuilding was arduous and Japanese quality was suspect and considered lacking. William Edwards Deming, an American, helped the Japanese develop a passion for design, quality, and innovation. The lessons Deming taught would later transform into Kaizen, a formalized process of continuous improvement.

Kaizen is one of my favorite concepts that we have infused into the culture at CaptiveAire. We were practicing continuous improvement long before I even heard the Japanese word for it. In our journey of constant improvement, we try every idea we can imagine. For example, we changed the production line five times in our Iowa plant as we worked to find the best method of manufacturing. Each time we rearranged the assembly lines and the storage of sheet metal, we achieved improvement, but it took extensive experimentation to achieve the efficiencies we enjoy today. We apply Kaizen to every aspect of our company, so that every detail, no matter how minor, is continuously in a state of development and improvement. This process is slow at first, but it soon builds a mentality of efficiency, quality, and pride.

GROWTH STRATEGIES

The most important role of the entrepreneur is to innovate and grow the enterprise. This growth not only includes products and services but also individual growth in everyone working for the enterprise. This means overcoming inertia and complacency, which occurs when people become stuck in one way of thinking or acting. This is consistently one of the most daunting leadership challenges. Conventional thinkers are abundant; excellent leaders who reject the status quo are scarce.

CaptiveAire is a dynamic company that is always transforming itself with new ideas for future growth. We continue to add products and capacity to our product line and to explore the technologies of the future. "Blockers," or stalwarts of the status quo, do not inhibit our growth; we do not allow them to stand in the way of new and potentially great ideas. We prefer the "lead, follow, or get out of the way" philosophy, which brings intellectual and physical energy to the enterprise and distinguishes the entrepreneurs from the bureaucrats. We respect the established processes and the engineers and innovators who came before us, but not to the point that we are unwilling to make radical changes based on evolving circumstances or new opportunities. We must be willing to discard even our own ideas and programs if a new and better idea comes along. Humility is crucial to the improvement cycle.

Sustaining constant growth is not a defined process, but rather requires thinking skills and a strong desire to improve. There are no simple road maps to help you build a business. If you can visualize the bigger, long-term goals it will be much easier to work through difficult and demanding near-term challenges. You must always keep an eye on the landscape, however, because it will change dramatically and constantly through the years.

It is critical to remember that a business enterprise must be able to perform many growth strategies simultaneously and over a long period of time. Development of a top quality, sustained enterprise is an honorable and important pursuit; excellent leadership is imperative to ensure the best possible execution.

KEY TAKEAWAYS:

- Make execution and outcomes your highest priority, not process.

- When making decisions, be bold but be right.

- Remember, you cannot control events but you can control your response and thus the outcome.

- Decentralize to avoid bureaucracy, streamline efficiencies, and provide exceptional service for the user.

- Foster autonomous employees; avoid handholding and suffocating management.

- Set the example for all employees from the top down—it is your responsibility as the leader to model the standard for everyone else.

- Work together as a team with complementary strengths to solve problems; however, remember that all achievement is rooted in the individual. Remove the blockers.

- Provide authentic praise to deserving employees early and often. Ensure they feel recognized and appreciated for their efforts.

- Maximize efficiency daily and improve continuously.

- Reject the status quo and conventional thinking in order to grow.

"Learning and innovation go hand in hand.
The arrogance of success is to think that what you
did yesterday will be sufficient for tomorrow."

WILLIAM POLLARD

CHAPTER SEVEN

INNOVATION

There is a strong tendency for businesspeople to become enamored with current methods or technologies. It's understandable that leaders are reluctant to make changes—it's expensive, and it's risky. Sometimes it flat out fails. When Coca-Cola changed its secret formula and introduced "New Coke" in 1985, for example, their loyal users rejected it outright. They didn't like the new taste, and they let the company know it. To their credit, Coca-Cola quickly reversed their decision and introduced "Classic Coke" (the old formula and the same Coke we drink today).

The initial decision by Coke was apparently based on faulty market research. If you're going to make a bold move, you better have reliable information. Even so, miscalculations will happen, but if you are nimble, you can quickly correct them.

At the same time, bold decisions have the capacity to change the world. The Apple iPhone redefined the market for a series of industries including camera, music, telephone, GPS, mobile hotspot, email, video, and web services. A decade ago phones were for making calls. Now it's almost unthinkable that call-only phones will even have a place in the market by the end of this decade. Apple has demonstrated the vulnerability of competitors; their disruptive products stun competitors even in unrelated industries. This demonstrates an important economic concept: competition is ubiquitous and can be stealthy.

Leaders of the most inventive companies realize that the inertia of the status quo undermines the future viability of any business, regardless of current sales growth or market acceptance of your product. Users understand and communicate their problems but rarely provide solutions—this is the mission of the entrepreneur.

REJECTING CONVENTIONAL WISDOM

On any given day, a nimble future entrepreneur may be thinking about and visualizing a new product, service, or technology that will render the current technologies obsolete.

Experience is important, but it can sometimes be a disadvantage when it comes to innovative problem solving, as mature companies and long-tenured personnel cling to the accepted norm. There are exceptions, but unfortunately they are rare. The concept of "best practices," made popular in the 1980s, has merit, but those standardized benchmarks must constantly be challenged, since they become the status quo. Even the very best ideas only have a limited life span. Non-intuitive ideas can become significant change agents, but it takes well-developed thinking skills to develop and harness new, commercially viable technologies and processes.

The Wright Brothers demonstrated this when they studied everything known about flight but in the end could not fly. When they eventually realized that part of the conventional science about flying was incorrect, they finally reached their breakthrough. They built a wind tunnel and began to experiment, expanding the length and reducing the width of the wings. Ultimately they also realized their controls for the airplane were not adequate. Many individuals were attempting flight but the

Wright Brothers used the scientific approach and continued experimenting and moving beyond mainstream knowledge until they were successful. They only spent about $1,000, while Samuel Langley, their contender, had a $50,000 government grant from the War Department, plus $20,000 from the Smithsonian Institution, and still failed to find a solution. As often happens, the best idea easily surpassed the better-funded competitor.

About twelve years ago, my engineer Bill Griffin came to me with unfortunate news. He had promised his wife that they would someday move to Pennsylvania, and the day had finally arrived. Our corporate office is in Raleigh, North Carolina, so he figured his career with CaptiveAire was over. Not wanting to lose exceptional talent, I quickly responded with, "Well, move to Pennsylvania and open your R&D lab there." This compromise was highly effective and Bill's contributions since then have been phenomenal and legendary. We have had similar successes with the transfer of our (now retired) VP of HR, Judy Nunnenkamp, to Charlotte, North Carolina, and Brady Ambrose, our head Application Engineer, to Utah. Through frequent communication and occasional visits to the corporate office, all of these arrangements have been highly successful despite their distance from our headquarters. Open-minded and counter-intuitive solutions are needed at all levels of a company, not just at the level of product design.

PROBLEM SOLVING

The process of creativity must begin with a review of the existing knowledge, but major success is achieved through bold new inputs and careful analysis as to how problems might be solved differently. Growth companies constantly learn, innovate, and improve, as they are never satisfied with existing technology.

Initially, several solutions to a problem may have equal weighting in the mind of the iconoclastic thinker. Each one must be explored, with all of the available information gathered and experimentation conducted before the final decision can be made. We continuously review products in the lab and in the field, tracking all failures in order to determine what can be improved. Our focus is sustainability under all conditions. A product may work well under lab conditions, but when installed in the "real world," new dynamics and stresses unfold, which is why beta testing is required.

Major innovations are hard to achieve, but we must constantly seek out opportunities. The entrepreneurial environment is not for risk adverse individuals. At CaptiveAire, we think in terms of disruptive products and services that radically change the marketplace and make a compelling case for the user to be a long-term customer.

In order to forge new products, technologies, and services, innovative entrepreneurs must assimilate information from a wide range of sources. At CaptiveAire, we constantly read industry publications to keep up with competitors and new research. We look at installations, including those of competitors, to find weaknesses or explore new ideas. We attend yearly product shows so that we are fully informed, and review any new or emerging technologies to determine if they can be useful in our product development process. We also learn from testing agencies and technical consultants and we frequently meet with architects and engineers to understand their challenges. This process must be robust and continuous, since one never knows when and where the next great idea will arise.

In this chapter I will highlight some of the major themes of our methods of innovation and some of the products that have been developed through these processes over the years. You will notice in these examples that brainstorming has a limited role, and groupthink is not part of the CaptiveAire process. The best ideas come from individuals, at many levels within the organization, and must be supported by leaders and team members. Innovation and passion, spurred by the entrepreneur, must permeate the thinking and actions of all employees at all times.

SOURCES OF NEW IDEAS

Innovation often comes from using disparate information; we study unrelated industries to determine different approaches and ways of thinking to shape our own methods. One example is a solution that came to us from the design of airplanes. The "Coanda effect," theorized by Henri Coanda, a Romanian aerodynamics developer, holds that moving air will be attracted to nearby hard surfaces. For airplanes, air flows over the wing and continues to move down wing flaps (providing aerodynamic lift) rather than shooting out laterally past the wing. Similarly, air that rises from cooking equipment tends to move toward the nearby wall, hugging the surface. We use this principle to design hoods, keeping the equipment snug to the wall, which helps capture the products of combustion until they enter the hood. This concept, though adopted from another industry, is critical to our application engineering and product design.

Along these same lines, we never hesitate to bring in new, younger minds to look at existing problems. If nothing else, they haven't yet learned their limits, which are often well established within industries. My father always stressed the importance of "the fast horses in the race" as an analogy, which illustrates the importance of talent, especially unbiased talent.

Julian Simon, author of *The Ultimate Resource,* argues that the limitless nature of the human mind is the greatest resource of all. The conventional wisdom is that knowledge is power, but unless it is harnessed and used at the right time and place, knowledge has no value.

Innovation begins with the known, but to move beyond this point we need new ideas. At CaptiveAire, we sometimes begin by thinking about how a product or technology might be if we began to design it from scratch. We also review how our products measure up with the best products in all types of industries. This is a high bar but it forces us to think differently and fosters deeper and more effective innovation.

RELYING ON TRUE SCIENCE

We extensively research the science behind every product idea. At CaptiveAire, we never follow industry trends simply because they are popular, but rather subject every component of our products to thorough testing procedures. By maintaining an open mind that is ordered to discerning the truth, we guarantee quality and performance and ensure customers that our products are reliable and proven in virtually all circumstances. Although this strategy is arduous, it is very helpful and always leads to long-term rewards. It is important to remember during this process that you may often find scientific outcomes that directly challenge the accepted status quo of your industry. You must have the courage to defy the status quo and stand out from the crowd. CaptiveAire advocates for our users, which fosters trust in our company and our products.

Around 2003, we faced one such situation, when UV (ultraviolet) hoods began to make a strong presence in the market. These kitchen hoods claimed to utilize ultraviolet light to break down and remove grease particles and odors. Although the product seemed promising, we did our research and decided not to manufacture it because we believed it was poor technology. We also learned that a major competitor had done a thorough investigation and determined that the technology was not adequate for kitchen ventilation systems. Some years later we had an outside testing lab conduct new testing and evaluations and they reached the same conclusion.

It is important to refrain from chasing a bad idea, regardless of its popularity. Our published research indicated that UVC (short wave) ray technology in commercial kitchen hoods was not commercially viable, and did not reach the threshold of quality and sustainability required for our industry. Our users appreciated that we went the extra mile to ensure that our products were designed in their best interest.

CUTTING COSTS IN UNIQUE WAYS

As I mentioned in Chapter 3, in late 1987 stainless steel prices were rising and I was concerned this increase would adversely affect our earnings and ability to continue to gain market share. We had traditionally used heavy 16-gauge stainless steel to make hoods, because stainless steel prices were low and stable. I began to think intensely about how to handle this challenge of increasing prices.

My initial thought was to lightweight (use less stainless steel in our products, making them lighter; similar to the car industry's reductions in weight over time) our hoods to reduce costs and remain competitive. I wrote down a series of ideas on how this could be accomplished—consistent with our quality and without an unfavorable perception in the market—and made some preliminary sketches. In our industry, a price increase in raw material is often passed along to the user. This was a prime opportunity to gain a major edge on the competition, increasing market share and profits without raising prices.

From my previous experience, I knew the modification could only be accomplished by a small group of committed engineers. I picked two young engineers to handle the design changes and two seasoned engineers to review the cutting efficiencies and cost savings of the stainless steel. The sense of urgency was critical. In January I gave the team a target of one month to complete the preliminary design. My father, Bill, and his silver foxes worked in the evenings to develop cost tables and determine whether we were meeting our goals for cost and material utilization. Working long hours, the design team turned out ideas and drawings, and the efficiency team reviewed every mechanical part with a goal of ninety-five percent efficiency of material usage.

We built models in our plant, which allowed us to structurally test and review the aesthetics, manufacturing process, and scale up issues (difficulties encountered in the initial manufacturing process). Our manufacturing team opposed the change but I felt strongly that this would be one of the most important innovations we had yet made. (Production workers and managers often oppose change because it initially impedes their work.) When finished, the lightweighting process effectively lowered costs, increased efficiency, and allowed us to reduce prices for our users at the same time that competitors were raising their prices. As a further benefit, lightweighting resulted in reduced shipping and installation charges for customers.

By late February, we were ready for production, and the same team helped us reconfigure our manufacturing process to implement the changes. The resulting product from the combined wisdom of both new and seasoned engineers was revolutionary and allowed CaptiveAire to substantially outpace the remaining pack of hood makers. It was one of the best and most important product decisions in the history of CaptiveAire. Our sales tripled during the next five years as a result of this innovation. I'm still not sure whether we would be where we are today had we not undertaken the lightweighting process.

Shortly after these new changes, I began a review of the actual type of metal we were using (as opposed to the weight). The entire industry used type 304 stainless steel, which is rich in nickel and chrome, two expensive alloys.

I contacted our metal manufacturer and asked him to look for and recommend a lower cost solution. He recruited a chemist who advised that we consider type 430 stainless steel. It is similar to 304 but uses lower quantities of chrome and nickel alloys, which were not needed for our application. The really good news was that 430 stainless steel cost less per pound, and was commonly used in Europe, but not in America. We located an excellent supplier in Mexico named Mexinox, which was owned by a German manufacturer. They agreed to supply the high quality stainless we needed. Tests were done in April and May, and by June we began production with the new metal. We held this innovation for twenty years before the foodservice industry standardized 430 stainless steel for most products.

Five years after we switched to the new metal, one of our salespeople asked why no other company had thought of these ideas. My answer was that they were simply not thinking, innovating, and looking for opportunities to improve. They were coasting on best or standard practices of the past. Our innovations allowed us to push past our competitors and establish confidence within the company, setting up the opportunity for further success down the road. When you're trying to beat competitors, it's important to get a head start before your competition catches up.

DEVELOPING NEW TECHNOLOGIES

New products and technologies are a passion and a prime reason for our growth at CaptiveAire, particularly for larger orders. "New technology" sales have accounted for fifty percent of our sales gain in recent years. It is never clear which technologies will dominate in the future. All CaptiveAire products, parts and service are under continuous review as we seek improved performance, reliability, and energy savings. Each year we introduce new technologies or upgrade existing products to incorporate new features and gain efficiency based on the dynamic performance of the products in the field, along with user feedback.

SIMPLE IDEAS, PHENOMENAL PRODUCTS

In 1975, I attended the Ansul Fire School in Marinette, Wisconsin. I was not anxious to attend, because at my job at the time we worked on commission, and my preference was to be in territory, selling.

The director of the fire school made a brief presentation as the course began. The first thing he stated was that the best agent to suppress fire is water. The statement was memorable, since we were there to learn how dry chemicals and other chemicals were effective firefighting agents. This was a seminal moment for me, not to be forgotten.

Many years later, at CaptiveAire, this basic concept resurfaced when we began to discuss the idea of a water-based fire suppression system (similar to a building sprinkler fire system), which would be electrically actuated. I was very confident about the idea, even though spraying water on a grease fire completely defied conventional wisdom.

Our VP of Engineering, Bill Griffin, responds quickly to new ideas. After we proposed the concept to him, he designed an in-hood sprinkler system and added a surfactant (a type of soap) to the water stream, which increased the firefighting capabilities of the water by reducing the surface tension between the water and grease, allowing the water to perform more effectively. Bill analyzed the shortfalls of the currently available chemical systems, and designed a superior product that utilizes modern technologies such as rate-of-rise detectors and electronic supervision and activation.

By August of 2008, we successfully ETL listed a self-cleaning hood with fire suppression for the duct and plenum (the area behind the filters), which we named CORE. This product was a revolutionary breakthrough in our industry, because fighting grease fires with water is extremely dangerous and was previously unsuccessful. CORE was a vastly improved solution that tackled numerous shortfalls of traditional chemical systems, which were messy and had high failure rates.

With the invention of CORE, we simplified fire suppression by using a rudimentary concept: water extinguishes fire. Because water can always be replenished, and because we guaranteed that our system was exceptionally reliable (which is critical during emergency situations), users immediately began to support CORE's design.

Our persistence and creativity in turning the market upside down and changing the long-held, conventional methods of fire suppression demonstrate that sometimes the simplest idea is the best idea. All that is required is the ability to think logically and creatively, while maintaining an open mind to find unique solutions to common problems.

A similar situation occurred in 2009 with the culmination of our modular design, when we had the idea of combining existing condenser technology with our Direct Fired Heater with DX Coil for cooling. This change allowed for the tempering (cooling) of hot air to a lower, more desirable temperature at a relatively low equipment and operating cost.

This product, known as the MPU (Modular Packaged Unit), has become the fasting selling new product in our history because it solves kitchen cooling issues at affordable utility costs. It is also illustrative of how important it is to rethink our approach. In this case we only lacked the controls and condenser to offer a complete solution that does not require field wiring or refrigeration connections.

In every aspect of our company, we aim to make complex ideas simple. There is no need for confusion or complications; most of life can be handled with very basic methods. As mentioned in Chapter 1, our mission is to "order the disordered." Other ways that we have simplified our processes and products include: factory-welded ductwork that provides for easy installation, single-point power connections that eliminate a tangle of endless power cords, and software systems that provide instant pricing quotes and detailed installation drawings for our sales crew.

Sometimes it is difficult to move beyond conventional methods and return to the basics, but in today's climate of maintaining greater and greater simplicity, removing complex processes and goods is key. Entrepreneurs who do not heed this lesson will soon despair as they will be surrounded by dissatisfied customers and unending complications that will hinder them from their true purpose—satisfying users and continuing to grow.

DISRUPTIVE INNOVATION

Clayton Christensen, professor at Harvard Business School, developed a concept called Disruptive Innovation, which he says "describes a process by which a product or service takes root initially in simple applications at the bottom of a market and then relentlessly moves up market, eventually displacing established competitors...an innovation that is disruptive allows a whole new population of consumers at the bottom of a market access to a product or service that was historically only accessible to consumers with a lot of money or a lot of skill." Think of the mainframe computer versus the personal computer, or the popular ridesharing app Uber, which had as its original slogan "Everyone's private driver." Uber allowed the common man access to a personal chauffeur on a daily basis.

Similarly, Balaji Srinivasin, a Silicon Valley CEO, champions the process of Exit vs. Voice. He describes Exit as the process by which a company innovates by exiting the market and taking an entirely new path, rather than trying to reform from within (which he calls Voice). Uber and Lyft are prime examples of Exit and disruptive innovation, because they bypassed the entire taxi industry and disrupted the status quo. Soon it will be difficult to find a traditional taxi anywhere because the convenience, price, and value of ride-sharing apps are quickly overtaking the industry.

At CaptiveAire, we force ourselves to think disruptively, continually asking ourselves how we can improve the industry in ways previously not considered. CORE is a great example of this type of thinking—we bypassed the chemical fire suppression industry and brought in a simpler and far more effective technology. The winners of the future will be those who Exit.

INNOVATION ACROSS ALL COMPONENTS

CaptiveAire expects the same quality from our suppliers that we expect from our end products, so we require rigid specifications from vendors to ensure performance. In some cases, suppliers are not responsive to our demands, so we must step in and tackle the problem ourselves.

A prime example is the fan industry. For many years, we could not achieve our product design requirements with existing fan manufacturers. We do not tolerate mediocrity so we decided to purchase FloAire, a small fan company, and alter its product according to CaptiveAire standards. The product upgrade included all of the features our users required: a welded tube to control grease in the bottom of the fan, latches on the fan cover so it could be removed without tools, a dramatically improved wheel welding to reduce noise, and structurally upgraded motor mounts to avoid vibration. Virtually every component of the fan was redesigned to improve aesthetics and structure, which led to its rapid acceptance. This important strategy—bringing the production of important components in house and redesigning them—along with more competitive pricing, helped us to dramatically expand our sales reach and enter new markets as a fan producer.

At the beginning of 2008, we acquired a grease filter technology known as Captrate, which was developed by a research group at Phillips Plastics Corporation in Wisconsin. Phillips marketed the product but was ultimately unsuccessful with it, so they offered to sell us the product, patent, and trade name. The new technology represented a dramatic breakthrough in capturing grease from the cooking process at the source. Captrate is a dual stage filter that captures ninety percent of grease particles that are seven microns or larger. In a few short years it has become the standard of the industry, with unit sales of over 50,000.

In 2009, we entered a new phase of product development, which included designing our own electronic controls. We hired Bill Glaub, who at one time had been a chief engineer for my brother Mike's company, POSITRAK. Bill had substantial expertise in electronic circuit board design. His first project was the forced high fire module for the IBT (Indirect Bent-Tube Fired Heater; a heater similar to the one in your home, but for commercial use), which supplied 10 volts DC for the first 17 seconds so the IBT would light-off (fire up) reliably in high fire. The new board guaranteed the proper fuel-air mixture for the lighting of the furnace, at a level of increased efficiency.

When this board was implemented, it became apparent how important proprietary electronic controls would be for our future. Next came a multi-stat (multiple thermostats) board for the EMS Energy Management System (Demand Ventilation). After that we designed the CORE board during our invention of the CORE system, which uses thermal detectors to supervise components such as water valves and actuators, activating at the presence of fire.

Custom electronic controls are transforming various aspects of our product development. Designing them in house gives us the capability to do exactly what we need them to do, and we have the ability to adjust or enhance them as needed (rather than working with outside vendors who may not be interested in making particular changes for us). Eliminating the need for third-party controllers also reduces costs.

The controls from 2009 are now being replaced with next generation purpose-built controls featuring even more advanced designs with expanded capabilities. All of the functionality of the earlier controls are now included on one board for increased efficiency.

The capabilities developed in the first decade of this century have allowed us to plot a new future of product development. All existing product lines have been reengineered and tested to meet the highest quality and performance standards.

Solid state controls have opened new opportunities as our engineers have focused on advanced software programs and the Internet of Things. Most of our products have the capabilities of 24/7 online monitoring and remote control with our proprietary CASLink software. We can now monitor facilities in real time, and if faults occur, we can diagnose and repair them rapidly.

Our introduction of the Paragon Dedicated Outdoor Air System represents a new era in our product development. The DOAS allows us to compete with the largest and best manufacturers in North America, providing an entire spectrum of heating and cooling solutions for commercial facilities.

MEETING USERS' NEEDS

One of the simplest ways to develop innovative ideas is by talking to your customers. We maintain good customer relationships, so we receive constant feedback about our products and the ways in which we can improve them and the overall user experience. We pay attention to our customers' financial needs as well so that we can provide the highest quality products at the most economical prices. We work tirelessly to provide all of our products and services to the best advantage of our users, and we do not "string them along" or blindside them with unneeded products or hidden costs. In addition, our customer relationships allow for a firsthand view of market trends, so we can constantly stay aware of our competition and the desires of our users.

The process of innovation is a continuously dynamic activity and requires continual vigilance. It is easy to grow complacent with current achievements and strategies, but successful entrepreneurs are those who know that they must sustain their businesses by constantly improving their offerings and services. Many firms soon become lethargic because they miss this point and fail to realize that all innovation is ephemeral.

CaptiveAire's strategy is formulated to achieve continuous improvement and innovation in all products and technologies. Surprisingly, this is not a burden, but rather is one of the most exciting aspects of growth. While quality is sometimes difficult to achieve, entrepreneurs must remember that the efforts to guarantee excellence will go a long way toward gaining and retaining loyal customers. Users who are extremely satisfied with your products and services ensure your future.

KEY TAKEAWAYS:

- Reject conventional wisdom. Stay open minded and consider all good ideas.

- Study ideas from all areas, even areas outside of your industry. You never know when a good idea may be applicable to your situation.

- Bring in young, unbiased talent to develop fresh new ideas. Don't worry about experience level. Young people often have very good ideas because they are not partial to the status quo.

- Develop your "ultimate resource," what Julian Simon calls the human mind. Learn and grow continuously to harness your full potential.

- Once you develop a new idea, test it out and experiment to confirm that it is in fact the best idea. Always beta test before rolling out full scale.

- When in doubt, keep it simple. There is no need to over-complicate ideas. Often, the simplest ideas are best.

- Harness Exit and disruptive innovation to gain the greatest potential for growth.

- Innovate and improve at all levels.

"Customers pay only for what is of use to them and gives them value. Nothing else constitutes quality."

PETER DRUCKER

CHAPTER EIGHT

FINANCE

Financial management was critical to survival in the first few years, because CaptiveAire began with a modest personal investment of only $1,300. Every decision had to make economic sense based on profit and cash flow.

The most important daily priority was to make sure we had all available funds in the bank. This meant picking up checks from customers if necessary to avoid having checks bounce the next day. That process continued throughout the first eight years of operation until we became financially solvent.

It takes a long time to build a solid business and reach financial stability. The key is to make and deploy capital effectively, while at the same time growing the creative potential of the enterprise. The most successful companies learn how to reduce and control costs as a core competitive edge. Too many entrepreneurs begin spending valuable cash flow after some early successes, which increases their vulnerability. Money spent frivolously or unproductively reduces profits, raises debt, and diminishes the chances of survival.

The learning curve in our first six years of struggle shaped the years that followed. The constant and difficult hurdles forced us to be good money managers and to think carefully about every dollar spent. We constantly worked to cut costs, improve quality, and reduce the selling price of our products to gain market share. Pricing had to be as low as possible, but consistent with achieving operating profits every month. This balance was important, because we could not survive without the cash flow, but growth was imperative to future cost efficiencies.

The financial meltdown of 2008 illustrates what can happen to businesses during difficult financial periods, no matter what their size. Bear Sterns and Lehman Brothers prospered for many years, but like so many businesses, they were both over-leveraged and failed in the 2008 financial meltdown.

By contrast, many of the most successful high-tech companies are cash rich and actually hoard cash to reduce the risk of market uncertainty. Companies such as Intel, Microsoft, Apple, and Cisco have strong balance sheets with large amounts of cash and very high liquidity. These strong financial positions increase management prerogatives in terms of acquisitions, new products, and expansion.

In this chapter I will share some of the most important financial concepts that have helped CaptiveAire achieve consistent growth over the years.

SOUND FINANCIAL PRACTICES

Sound financial practices are imperative to the survival and growth of a company. Balance sheets should be clean and based on GAAP (Generally Accepted Accounting Principles). Accounting statements should fairly represent the operating earning and financial position of a company. Managers want to present their results in the best possible light, of course, but unfortunately this provides incentives to violate accounting principles.

When sound accounting principles are followed, business owners have good information with which to make decisions. Conversely, if the accounting numbers are gamed, serious trouble may result in the long run. Dishonest accounting practices can include sending out bills for work not completed or shipped, failing to report all expenses in a given accounting period, or misrepresenting the capitalization of operating expenses. Delayed write-offs are destructive because they ruin the credibility of your financial reporting. Violation of the standard principles increases risk and is self-deceptive. It takes a team of strong character to maintain accurate accounting records.

UNDERSTANDING THE NUMBERS

Effective entrepreneurs understand the numbers themselves and review them regularly to improve and be cognizant of current operations. A good financial team is important but the leader of the company must also have a thorough knowledge of financial accounting.

I mentioned that in 1982, our CFO, Bill Francis, informed me that we were losing money ($50,000 in the first quarter). Our sales were lower than expected (only $84,000 in February and $396,000 for the entire first quarter), and it was a wake-up call. I immediately resumed my role as the leader of the sales teams, and second quarter sales rose to over $620,000, while third quarter sales were in the $630,000 range. We returned to profitability and have not lost money in any subsequent quarter since. Close attention to the financials and swift action saved the company.

Peter Drucker, the renowned management consultant and author, once said, "By the time you recognize problems in the financial statements, the hour may be very late." With that in mind, we review general and administrative expenses monthly, with specific individuals responsible for each segment of the business. This process is regular and continuous, and we sometimes have to make very difficult decisions based on our reviews. It is critical for the leader to sort out ineffective programs and people when they are uncovered; failure to act burns cash flow and degrades progress.

Outside experts, such as CPAs, attorneys, and insurance agents, can be important resources for an entrepreneur. Problems with tax authorities and employment laws often arise because the entrepreneur is moving forward with growing the business without understanding certain tax or legal requirements or implications. Even before Bill Francis came to us, we had some outside advisors who provided their services at reasonable fees. We used independent CPAs who provided expert advice on accounting procedures and systems, and attorneys to handle our incorporation and act as our legal counsel.

Even now, after so many years of practice, we still regularly rely on the expertise of outside advisors. With his background in finance as a former controller for Owens Illinois International, board member and my brother-in-law, Harry Silletti, has a knack for analyzing financial opportunities and shortfalls in our system. Harry spends one week per quarter with us reviewing all aspects of the operation, including budgets, costs, and performance data for possible improvement. We evaluate:

- Monthly company and plant financial performance (to discuss marketing and product pricing strategies to improve volume or enhance profitability of the company)

- Monthly production trends by plant (to monitor productivity gains over the years)

- Financial performance of all sales regions (to identify unfavorable trends in order to provide corporate attention and help to the underperforming sales regions)

- Annual trends in sales by state (to evaluate options for adding new plant or sales operations)

BUDGETING FOR SUCCESS

Budgeting and estimating must be core skills, developed as early as possible in the life of a company. I cannot emphasize this enough: conservative cash flow management is critical. The finance team at CaptiveAire is always respected as part of the management team. Financial controls are taken very seriously and exceptions are carefully thought out.

The CFO plays a key role in cash management and profits and must be allowed to rein in expenses. Without a governor, costs can get out of control quickly. Every member of our management team, as well as every employee, is keenly aware of cost control. Budgets, which in our minds are maximum spending targets, are not always shared with operations but are used by my CFO and myself as a roadmap to evaluate requests for new and routine spending. We do provide guidelines, but we have learned that providing fixed budgets tends to increase spending.

The process of reducing costs and completing projects below the budget has become a major competitive advantage for us. CaptiveAire has been the low-cost producer in our industry for as long as we've been in business, and this is one of the main contributors to the growth in our market share.

Very high employee productivity has been instrumental in our efforts to cut costs as well. We utilize new technologies and stress continuous improvement, which leads to higher production by each employee. For example, in 1981, a hood welder produced about two hoods per week. By 2003, our best producers averaged thirty-five hoods per week with assistance from a pre-assembly team. Our process changed again in 2004, and we now produce thirty hoods per day, per plant, with a relatively small team.

LOANS AND DEBT

Despite the best efforts to keep spending in check, when a firm begins to grow rapidly and needs more capital, it is sometimes necessary to seek temporary funds from outside sources.

Banks operate differently than venture capitalists, and are a safer bet for most entrepreneurs. They charge interest only, usually up to a few points over the prime rate or LIBOR (LIBOR is a benchmark short term rate). Since a loan involves a high degree of trust, most banks evaluate the personal character of the principals during the loan process. They will need to be assured of both your competency and your integrity. It is imperative that you gain their confidence with good, reliable performance and realistic expansion plans.

You will recall that in 1981 we had about $300,000 in short term bank debt. The goal was to develop a plan to pay it down as rapidly as possible. The only way to do this was to generate free cash flow with sales growth and cost controls. It is important to develop specific targets for debt reduction and challenge yourself to meet them. CaptiveAire paid off its debt in the early 1990s, which then allowed us to expand with internally generated funds, a major luxury for any entrepreneur.

In those days there was a lot of excitement about the stock market and IPOs. It can be tempting to think about taking a company public in order to raise funds externally for expansion. An associate of mine at that time, Hugh Carr, stressed to me the importance of never going public for any reason because of the many challenges he had encountered. He was the CEO of a NYSE publicly traded company named Trion, Inc., located in Sanford, North Carolina. He related the challenges of managing a public company, especially the frustration of being stalked by Wall Street analysts. He was eventually fired by the board, which turned out to be a fatal error. The trajectory of the company deteriorated after Hugh's departure, and eventually Trion was sold to another publicly traded company.

My own Uncle Bill, who I mentioned earlier, went through a similar experience when his Servomation Corporation in New York City deteriorated in 1970. He was a determined man, so he started again and created an entirely new venture, Serex Services, Inc. Fortunately, it was quite successful and he led it until he sold it upon his retirement when he was in his mid-80s. I was convinced by these cautionary tales, and never thought about going public.

These days, more U.S. companies are choosing to remain private to avoid the massive regulations imposed by the government and the meddling of investors, most of which are temporary. In addition, it is a complex process that is both time-consuming and costly. There are now half as many publicly traded companies as there were in the mid-90s. Most of the decline is due to the low number of new listings. Startups are instead turning to other forms of capitalization that allow them to maintain control, or they are selling their companies outright once they reach profitability. I personally detest regulation and red tape, so I don't ever plan to take CaptiveAire public.

Entrepreneurs are risk takers, but they must manage risk prudently and become sharp resource managers. Careless or reckless entrepreneurs rarely survive in the long run.

FROM THE TOP DOWN

People tend to be either savers or spenders, often based on the financial concepts they learned within their families. When I was growing up, money was always in short supply and the list of needs was long. Although my dad made a decent salary as an engineer, he had ten mouths to feed and often had to decide which bills to pay.

While at times my siblings and I felt somewhat deprived, we overcame those feelings by working hard and earning and saving our own money. I would not trade my early experiences with monetary strain for anything; my parents taught me the frugality that enabled me to save my way to personal financial comfort. Many folks ask me why I don't spend more money on myself, but I merely respond that my avocations are my fulfillment.

Given today's economic climate, lean operations are a necessity, but I have long practiced austerity, due in large part to my childhood experiences. CaptiveAire's sales per employee are tracked annually as a measure of efficiency and viability in the market. Due to our resourcefulness, we have one of the best rates in the HVAC industry. It takes ingenuity to remain lean, because managers will often ask for more resources than are absolutely necessary. Adding too many people in a group frequently leads to lower aggregate output, and it can degrade service. Modern technology allows the best decision makers to be highly productive with very small staffs.

My view is that it's more important to keep the business under good financial control than to expand too rapidly, take on partners, and borrow money, all of which can increase risk and operational complexity. Operating a business debt-free is a great luxury and keeps the creditors from controlling the business.

The development of a conservative culture starts at the top, with the founder and CEO. The entrepreneur sets the financial tone for the entire company. Maintaining a frugal lifestyle was important to me, which meant taking only the minimum salary necessary to meet expenses. As a result, from the very beginning, I took just what I needed, about $30,000 in the beginning. It was actually slightly less than I'd been earning at my last job, but reinvesting in the company to ensure its future was most important to me.

This financially conscious attitude must be reflected in all levels of management. You must hire managers who embrace your cost-saving techniques to ensure the best possible execution and follow-through. These methods will then funnel down to all employees within the company.

STRONG FINANCIAL MANAGEMENT

As I mentioned, when our bank required us to hire a CFO as a condition for a major bank loan in 1981, I was reluctant, but not bullheaded. It was the right move at the right time. The decision seemingly required the violation of the lean principle, but sometimes investments must be made to achieve growth. Bill Francis proved to be one of our very best investments.

Many small businesses fail to grow beyond about $2 to $5 million, because they never develop a professional level of management. Often the first two or three employees end up taking on responsibilities for which they are not capable or prepared. The classic example is the receptionist who also does the bookkeeping and the human resource work. This is fine when the company has five or fifteen employees. But there comes a point at which a company's needs grow in size and complexity far beyond what the initial employees or systems can handle, and then you must recruit higher-level professionals and introduce formal systems. Hiring a CFO was one of the best strategic management decisions in the history of CaptiveAire. It is important to reiterate that although it was not my idea, I was able to see the wisdom in the recommendation.

NEGOTIATING WITH VENDORS

At CaptiveAire, we have a unique relationship with our suppliers, and we work very hard to get the lowest prices on every item we buy. We look for supplies that bring us the most value and we seek out machine tools that make processes smoother, safer, and more efficient. There are times when providers do not keep up with the market requirements, be it electrical switching devices, fabricated parts, or new technologies. When this is the case, it opens up opportunities for new vendors.

We use sole source vendors with whom we have long-term relationships, some over twenty-five years. This may seem counterintuitive, but by awarding all of the business to one supplier, we gain a price advantage, and the vendor knows that they must take very good care of our account to maintain this status. Close vendor relationships can be very productive, provided that both parties negotiate in good faith and maintain a fair balance.

This strategy has some obvious risks, which we believe are outweighed by the rewards. Our vendors have huge and growing sales volumes, which they protect with great service and low prices.

You often hear the trite phrase, "You get what you pay for." If this were true, there would be no need for negotiations or discerning buyers. A more correct statement is, "You get what you negotiate for based on information and knowledge of your industry." In many cases we have offered huge contracts to successfully drive down costs. Economies of scale can be more important than patents in the manufacturing business. From the beginning we recognized the importance of scale, which never before existed in our industry since most manufacturers were relatively small.

CASH FLOW MANAGEMENT

Profits are not the same thing as cash flow, but they are too often confused. If you don't have cash in the bank, you can't operate, regardless of your profitability. Cash flow management is one of the most important determinations of business success and viability. In 1980, we were making a profit but our cash flow was terrible and we had to dramatically reduce expenses.

Every important decision should be weighed with cash flow in mind, including new hires, capital expenditures, and operating expenses. Harry Silletti engrained this philosophy into the CaptiveAire mentality.

Operational disciplines are critical to profitability and cash flow. The cash flow discipline also represents a competitive edge because with adequate cash flow, management can afford to take prudent risks. Since the 2008 recession, after learning the hard way, many businesses are now building cash reserves for future uncertainties.

CORRECT PRICING AND SIMPLIFIED FORMULAS

Some of our competitors charge excessively high prices. It was fair to say that before our entry into this business, users were overpaying for ventilation systems, which spelled opportunity for CaptiveAire. Interestingly, there were some who thought we should charge more for our products. I rejected this strategy to focus on the long run, which allowed us to gain market share every year. For example, sales expanded from $6.6 million in 1986 to $21 million in 1991 in large part due to our low pricing.

High prices can mask inefficiencies within an enterprise, creating opportunities for more nimble competitors. Peter Drucker made it clear that maximum profits are achieved by correctly pricing a product, which means pricing at a level that maximizes long-term sales and profits. We take full advantage of his wisdom in all of our pricing strategies.

Most companies expend an enormous amount of time and money tracking labor and material costs—what is commonly referred to as "cost accounting." Traditional cost accounting requires the review of time sheets or logins as well as the analysis of allocations of overhead to labor and material. Even when software is used, it consumes many man-hours and often becomes the priority. Rupp, under its former management, was greatly hindered by its accounting software, so we abandoned it quickly after our acquisition. The finance team should facilitate, not hinder, growth.

We devised a simple system for pricing standard products that requires little time and is quite accurate. Our pricing strategy maintains profit margins by using standard material and labor costs as a percentage of the selling price of each product. The accuracy of this method is verified monthly by comparing the actual costs to standard costs that are charged to the financial statements each month. After comparing, significant variances are investigated and prices are adjusted if needed.

The advantage of using simple multipliers is that all products can be easily adjusted for market conditions. Multipliers are versatile and can vary by product, depending on estimated labor, the competitive price in the market, the manufacturing process, and future expectations of cost reductions.

Electronic bill of materials (BOMs) for each product compile all material costs, which are electronically tracked and linked to current costs from vendors. These functions require enterprise software, which updates component costs in real time. Automated software keeps management aware of cost changes, allowing us to always be armed with accurate information at all times.

DECENTRALIZED PROFIT CENTERS

At CaptiveAire, every operating division has its own monthly profit and loss (P&L) statement. This includes all one hundred sales regions, six plants and sixty service divisions. Individual P&Ls allow for local decision making on fund allocations, enabling regional managers to make adjustments according to the needs in their markets. We also generate aggregate sales and manufacturing P&Ls. These statements are analyzed with reports designed to highlight key data points. Individual managers receive copies of these reports, encouraging better performance.

ECONOMICS IN ACTION

As mentioned at the beginning of this book, I have a passion for free market economics and was honored to learn under the mentorship of Dr. Peterson, an excellent professor and economist. He helped me to understand the value of a few key principles and advised me on how to implement them at CaptiveAire. I now speak often about the importance of cooperation, transaction cost, opportunity cost, comparative advantage, and Say's Law, which states that supply creates demand.

The close correlation between sound economic principles and the practice of great business strategies is often overlooked. Business leaders often talk about free market economic principles but at times they fail to deeply know and implement these principles even in their own industries. When understood and used properly, these concepts can have a profound impact on the success of a business.

Cooperation allows a group of varying perspectives and opinions to work together and solve problems for the greater good. Employees at CaptiveAire can (and do) disagree, but in the end we make the best decisions consistent with quality and cost. Cooperation produces a work setting that allows top professionals to thrive and accelerates the decision making imperative to a growing business. It facilitates greater outcomes by focusing creative energy productively and precludes turf wars. When cooperation is low, meetings are long and the decision-making process is hindered.

Transaction costs encompass all of the costs involved in making an exchange, including total costs, implicit costs and unit costs of time, effort, and other resources. Specialization, division of labor and technology have helped reduce transaction costs over time. At CaptiveAire, we are committed to reducing transaction costs as much as possible in order to lower prices for our customers. For example, when manufacturing, we streamline processes to reduce labor and negotiate for the best supplier costs whenever possible. These savings then get passed on to our users.

Opportunity costs are the costs of the opportunities left behind when choosing between two or more potential options. Our time is our most precious resource; we must use it wisely. Too often, people waste time or fail to allocate it properly. If employees are participating in fruitless meetings, conferences, or idle chatter in the office, growth is not being accomplished. Individuals who work hard and prioritize their time will produce good outcomes, allowing their contributions and careers to flourish. Every decision must be made with opportunity costs in mind.

Comparative advantage is the upper hand a company has when it is able to produce a good at a lower cost or at higher quality than a competitor. This differs from competitive advantage, because comparative advantage is an inherent advantage—it cannot be overcome. Another company may have a different comparative advantage than yours does, but it can never overcome the advantage you have. Opportunity cost is key to comparative advantage—you must choose the opportunities that leverage your comparative advantage the most. One example of this at CaptiveAire is the decision to locate plants regionally rather than having one central plant for all markets. The ability to ship our products more quickly and at a cheaper rate gives us a comparative advantage over our competitors who ship throughout the country from one central source.

Jean-Baptiste Say asserted that "supply creates demand," which is now known as Say's Law. The best and most innovative companies understand this law well. Rather than wait for consumers to desire a new product, innovators develop an excellent product, which naturally leads to demand. None of our customers asked us to create CORE Fire Protection, but now that they see how effective and reliable it is, they wish to have it their kitchens. The entrepreneur plays a unique role in shaping the future of our world, as supply creates consumer demand and drives the future forward.

I am forever grateful to Dr. Bill Peterson and a host of others who have helped me to master these important economic concepts. These principles are rarely taught in school, but they're imperative for the success of any entrepreneurial organization. Entrepreneurs must understand the implications of economics in the marketplace and within their organizations and make decisions that will benefit their companies and their users.

STRONG FINANCIAL MANAGEMENT

Financial management is a core competence of CaptiveAire, stemming from my own personal interests in finance that began in my childhood. It is critical to manage cash flow effectively and to keep debt low to ensure that the company has the financial strength needed to meet all current and future challenges. We constantly analyze data so that we have a thorough understanding of all of our expenses. This leads to reductions in both direct and general and administrative (G&A) costs, making our products more competitive.

Patience is not an innate virtue for entrepreneurs but the reality is that it often takes up to ten years to establish a strong growth business. Some of the best businesses in America are run by the founding entrepreneurs, or their families, for thirty years or longer. James Maynard of Golden Corral and the Cathy family of Chick-fil-A are prime examples. Many industries flourish under private long-term management, avoiding the short-term focus held by most public companies.

Simplicity, like frugality, is a financial virtue. It requires careful consideration of strategies and next moves. Continuous review helps to reduce bad decisions and improves outcomes, while forcing the leader to be well grounded in financial reality.

One minute we are on top of the world, and the next we are hit hard by new challenges and worries about the future. The lows can be mitigated with a commitment to maintaining a strong financial position. Sometimes we must sacrifice growth for financial stability. Solid financial management provides the maximum growth opportunities for the entrepreneur.

KEY TAKEAWAYS:

- Maintain integrity and sound financial practices at all times. Accurate data is imperative for sound decision making.

- Understand the numbers. Do not outsource decision making to the "experts." Utilize their counsel but make sure you understand and make decisions based on that understanding.

- Maintain a budget and stick to it. Ensure that you always have adequate cash flow to pay the bills.

- Manage risk prudently. Avoid debt and loans as much as possible. Strong cash reserves ensure security, regardless of market conditions.

- Negotiate and cut costs as much as possible without harming quality.

- Understand the economic principles of cooperation, transactional cost, opportunity cost, comparative advantage, and Say's Law. Use these principles to guide all management decisions.

- Maintain strong financial management over a long period of time to gain financial stability.

"The only source from which an entrepreneur's profits stem is his ability to anticipate better than other people the future demand of the consumers."

LUDWIG VON MISES

CHAPTER NINE

SALES AND MARKETING

Finding new users and providing superior integrated engineering solutions is critical to growth. This process is relentless and requires finding new territories and market segments.

As you have learned, for most of CaptiveAire's sales history, I have been the sales leader and have focused on growth. Sales management is one of my most important responsibilities. It requires a high level of curiosity and creativity. Due to the technical nature of our product, marketing and advertising have a limited value, so sales efforts are a necessity.

Sales, at its most basic level, is about executing a few basic concepts correctly, including:

- Finding new users in a dynamic market as some longer, tenured users exit.

- Offering the best possible price the first time, and finding a way to close orders.

- Keeping in touch with your customer. The "out of sight, out of mind" rule applies. Maintaining good relationships is key to customer loyalty and continued sales.

- Continuously providing timely product and market information that has value to customers. Users expect salespeople to keep them informed, not vice-versa.

- Providing immediate, complete, and stellar service with great empathy for users.

- Solving any problem or challenge of the user. This is a primary responsibility of all sales engineers.

FANATICAL FOCUS ON THE CUSTOMER

"The purpose of business is to create and keep a customer," said Peter Drucker, and this has always been the touchstone of my approach. The customer is sovereign in the free market and is the undisputed boss of every entrepreneur and employee of the enterprise. Customers want what is of use to them, and nothing more. They demand value, utility, quality, and solutions, or they will not buy.

Customers' values are in constant flux, as are tastes. Due to customer demands, the supermarket has replaced the iceman, milkman, and the bread man. The big boxes have replaced the small shops, and online giants are seriously threatening the big boxes. The high-end organic and locally grown green grocers have cut away at the large grocery chains. It's a never-static landscape; businesses either adapt or fall by the wayside.

Many businesses offer products or services that are equal to or only marginally better than those of their competitors. Matching the competition is an untenable approach to growth and is simply not enough to establish or sustain a business. Aiming to be the best option for customers is the only way to truly succeed.

EXCEEDING EXPECTATIONS

Companies that find every possible way to pleasantly surprise users are the potential winners in any market. Customers appreciate vendors, suppliers, and service providers who anticipate their needs and always have their best interests in mind.

Ultimately, business policies do not work unless they meet the needs of the user. Chick-fil-A has mastered this concept; their employees are always looking for ways to go above and beyond to make the customer experience a satisfying one. From simple policies such as offering freshly ground pepper on salads and placing fresh flowers at every table, to reengineering the drive-thru process to allow for a faster and more personal visit, Chick-fil-A has found numerous ways to offer a superior customer experience far above the usual expectations of a fast food restaurant. They consider serving and giving to be their primary mission, and as a result have garnered incredible customer loyalty. On any given day at most Chick-fil-A locations across the U.S., you can find packed restaurants and long drive-thru lines filled with eager customers asking for more.

Achieving this type of customer-centric culture requires flexibility and nimble, dynamic managers, not complex policies and rigid administration. Many large companies struggle with this because their numerous bureaucratic policies restrict employees' freedom to serve. Startup companies are more flexible, but are often unable to achieve sustained growth because they miss an important point: the user makes the final decision about whether a business is successful, not the entrepreneur. Customers can afford to be very demanding in a market economy and they will not accept excuses. Ted Fowler, former president of Golden Corral, often points out that "customer loyalty is the absence of a better choice."

Thus, it is important to remember that exceeding expectations must become the norm within your company; it cannot be an occasional or "sometimes" policy. For example, if a customer calls their favorite restaurant for a reservation, they expect the restaurant to accommodate them regardless of how busy they are. If the restaurant fails to meet their needs, they are forced to look for another restaurant, which might turn out to be their new favorite place to eat. Delivering the best possible experience every time is the requirement. You only get one chance to fail a customer in a marketplace that is competitive.

Our total focus at CaptiveAire is to rise above the competition and provide excellent customer service from first contact, with rapid-response quotes, detailed dynamic submittals, and fast shipments. We aim to offer the "wow" factor every time, in every aspect of a customer's experience, and we know that you can't substitute style for substance.

ATTRACTING THE RIGHT PEOPLE

As the ultimate head of sales, one of the most important challenges is to find and retain the right salespeople. At CaptiveAire, over time, we have created an environment conducive to attracting the very best sales personnel in the industry. Most of our new salespeople are graduate engineers. We do consider equivalent experience, but eighty percent of our sales team is comprised of engineers. This ensures that we deliver the best possible customer service because our salespeople truly understand the technical considerations of kitchen ventilation, and are able to design the best possible system for the user's specific requirements.

We prefer to hire recent graduates with five or fewer years of work experience so that we can avoid the bad habits and poor practices often found in experienced individuals. We require our new salespeople to go through a rigorous training process so that we can form excellent sales engineers from the ground up. Since this program requires such a large investment on our part, we want to be absolutely certain that participants are top-notch individuals with huge potential and excellent character.

We typically hire about ten to twenty new sales engineers per year, but these spots are highly competitive, with the number of applicants ranging from ten to fifty per position depending on the position location. Our interview process is lengthy, allowing us to get to know candidates quite well and allowing them to get a comprehensive view of CaptiveAire, our expectations, and our culture. This saves enormous time and energy later on by avoiding employee turnover. We want to make sure we make the right decision for us, but we also want employees who will fit in and be happy in the long run.

We make it clear up front that we are looking for highly motivated, aggressive, and dedicated salespeople. They must be prepared to make their jobs a priority and be willing to service users beyond the normal business day when necessary.

Candidates must also be self-reliant and able to work at a high level independently. With our sales team decentralized, salespeople must operate as if self-employed, although we do provide strong operating procedures from the corporate office. We issue product application guidelines that must be followed to ensure that quality standards are achieved. Since we rarely have company-wide sales meetings, our constant emails, occasional telephone calls, and monthly webinars help disseminate these management, engineering, and strategy concepts to our regional sales offices across the country. Sales recruits must be prepared to use these resources and embrace our unique structure and environment.

In Chapter 6, I referenced Jim Collins' concept of getting the right people on the bus. This idea is supported throughout all steps of our sales hiring process, because sales are what drive our company forward. It is essential that we obtain and keep the highest quality people on our team in order to secure our future success.

SALES TRAINING

Once hired, our new salespeople, called EITs (Engineers in Training), enter a year long program of extensive training and instruction at a plant, our R&D facility, regional office(s), and with a field service team, if available. The goal is for each new individual to learn our technologies and products; understand our manufacturing, ordering, installation, and service processes; and master application engineering. In addition, they learn the expectations and nuances of our company culture and sales methods, allowing them to develop the traits needed to succeed in our company.

Most of our training is hands-on and interactive, which is very effective. Developing excellent judgment and attention to every detail requires considerable experience and repetitive exposure. Throughout the initial 12-month training and beyond, the EITs learn in their regional office, where an experienced regional sales manager and local technicians mentor them. Individuals learn at a level based on their ability and motivation. Most learn quickly if they apply themselves and strive to improve daily.

From the start, we encourage our EITs to spend one hour each day studying our products, industry, technologies, and engineering. Self-motivated employees who take this continuous learning process seriously will become product experts in fewer than three years. We also encourage our EITs to learn about economic principles that impact their performance.

New recruits join our industry group, ASHRAE (American Society of Heating, Refrigerating, and Air Conditioning Engineers). Most ASHRAE chapters provide technical seminars at their monthly meetings and annual conferences. These events provide EITs an opportunity to meet mechanical engineers and contractors who are our users.

Our new salespeople bring energy and ideas, strengthening our team. We see it as our job to transform this raw talent into excellence through our robust training and formation. It is surprising how quickly individuals form good habits that are not easily broken.

INDEPENDENT SALES OFFICES

Our sales regions are completely empowered to operate independently with self-reliance. Each office designs, sells, sets prices, services, and handles any local issues without outside interference. Common opinion may refute this setup as difficult to manage, but we do not find this to be the case. We follow several principles that enable us to manage a large sales force with no sales manager (besides myself) and minimal administration:

- IT provides an array of software programs, including point-of-sale quotations, automated submittal data and drawings, and secondary programs for duct designs and drawings.

- All scheduling is based on short lead times and is fully automated and updated by tracking emails (similar to UPS and FedEx).

- Product quality is high, reducing field issues.

- Manufacturing is decentralized, to the local or regional level. The regional sales teams deal directly with their respective plant for any issues.

- Regional sales teams can contact anyone in the company for help including me, which is routine. We do not have bureaucracy interfering with our sales operations.

- Our personnel are trained to immediately address problems and fix them. We do not tolerate management or engineering delays.

- Any team member, whether in finance, accounting, engineering, manufacturing, sales operations, or human resources, can provide feedback or correction to regional offices. This affords great teamwork to serve our users.

Sales regions' efforts are augmented by a small sales support team and a few administrators at the corporate office who create presentations, help with application engineering, work with national accounts and buying groups, and resolve user or distribution issues. Approximately once per quarter, I call each sales region and talk to the regional manager to address any issues, identify difficulties, and develop ways our corporate team can help.

The strength of our direct sales force program remains one of our most important competitive strategies today. Many competitors have tried to replicate our program, with minimal success.

TECHNOLOGY STREAMLINES PROCESSES

A great deal of quality control is embedded in our ordering software, which we named NOLA. NOLA is based on the original CASPER system that my father designed, and was developed through the efforts of Janis Braslins, now our VP of Systems Architecture, and my son Randy. Randy worked with a designer to create a user-friendly interface very quickly over a few weekends, and Janis developed the back end of the system. We now have an entire team dedicated to maintaining and updating NOLA weekly.

NOLA is extremely helpful in ensuring a quality system design by automatically generating prompts for application engineering standards. Defaults let the specifier know the best choice for various parts of the system such as hoods, fans, filters, etc. These choices can be overridden based on user preference or design specifications, but the software has built-in safeguards against unwise or marginal engineering.

NOLA also generates quotes, submittals, and drawings from the ordering process. This allows our sales teams to provide real time quotes and drawings, which is revolutionary in our industry. NOLA creates a permanent file for all jobs, including original engineering and manufacturing notes, and all service after the sale including pictures.

This software, while a continuous challenge to update and maintain by our IT team, is a huge benefit to our sales team. It greatly streamlines processes and ensures that we consistently design the best systems for our users. As in every industry, evolving technology has greatly simplified and improved everyday processes. Software investments, especially when proprietary, are large, but can provide huge dividends in the long run, escalating companies to a modern level and allowing for tremendous growth potential. NOLA continues to be a key advantage for us in our industry.

MARKETING

During the startup and initial phases of the company, our entire focus was on sales, which is the best way to begin many companies, especially those on a small budget. If you have a novel idea and excellent service and/or high value products, word of mouth is the most powerful marketing tool available.

In our seventh year (1983), we made our first brochure on kitchen hoods and included a logo. The following year our marketing expanded to include a catalog. I personally never felt the need for this type of collateral material because of my strong sales orientation. However, our sales team believed that we needed a catalog similar to our competitors' material in order to grow. While these two publications, as well as some business cards and stationery, were somewhat helpful, it is amazing how much business we developed without any formal marketing beyond these few items.

As we entered the 1990s, our sale teams demanded more catalogs, which became a yearly undertaking. Since we were growing quickly, by the time catalogs were printed, they were partially out of date. We struggled with this problem until the evolution of the Internet, when the gap between current designs and market information was finally reconciled.

As mentioned in Chapter 4, we have acquired several competitors over the years. Though we still don't invest heavily in marketing, we have often chosen to retain our acquisitions' marketing strategies, as these sectors have strong industry contacts and the ability to gain market share for our products.

In terms of ad campaigns, periodically we ran some magazine ads and attended national shows, but after 1987, these became ancillary marketing tools rather than primary ones. We were gaining tremendous sales momentum, and this all but precluded the need for advertising.

In 2008 we realized that although CaptiveAire was well known as a manufacturer of commercial kitchen ventilation systems, users did not know that we also produced make-up air systems, fans, and electrical controls. We began a small advertising program called System 10 (the ten products that made CaptiveAire a fully integrated kitchen ventilation system) to retool our image and reach more users. In recent years, we've changed the name of this campaign to The Complete Solution, emphasizing CaptiveAire's focus on integration and our complete system approach.

The real power behind CaptiveAire's marketing lies in our customer webinars, product training sessions, videos, website, and local display centers.

Our philosophy of marketing includes:

- Focus your attention on improving your products and service. If you provide a good offering, the product will attract buyers.

- Spend very little on advertising; you only need enough ads to keep the user reminded of your brand.

- Rely on word of mouth—this is a very powerful concept in sales growth.

- Show the product in person when possible. In our industry, having the ability to see and interact with the product before purchasing is rare.

- Use available technology extensively, such as the company website and instructional videos.

DISPLAY CENTERS

Great ideas do not come along often but we must always maintain an open mind and seek the next good opportunity. Our thinking becomes stale without new inputs, which can hinder our chances of success if we are not open-minded.

In 2009, one of our customer groups requested that we ship a hood with a utility cabinet to a hotel in Chicago, where they were holding a sales meeting. I was not in favor of the idea due to the expense and time involved, given that the display would only be used for a few hours. But I am always open to new ideas, even when I am not necessarily convinced they are sound. We shipped the hood to the hotel and they temporarily set it up in a conference center for the review of the sales engineers.

To my surprise, the engineers and sales people who attended the presentation indicated that having the product onsite made it a much more real and productive experience. It was a very successful meeting and I learned a profound lesson. Most people want to see, touch, and experience the product firsthand, which is why product displays have played a big part in the success of big box retailers.

Historically, in our industry it was customary to invite users and engineers to the factory for a tour and product demo. Over time, most users began to refrain from taking the time to visit factories. National product shows helped, but the audience was limited and the shows lasted for only a few days each year. As I pondered the positive results of the display in Chicago, I developed an entirely new idea: local display centers.

What if we had a full-blown display of all of our key products in every major market in the country? The cost and challenge would be high, but I knew that this might be a marketing idea that could significantly change the industry.

Our first display centers opened in Orlando, Minneapolis, and Miami in 2010, and they were quickly successful. I immediately determined that we needed a national rollout of this idea, which would include at least fifty major locations throughout North America. After five years, we now have fifty centers open, with a steady stream of new locations in the works. At each display center, we are able to demonstrate products, perform tests, and show how our monitoring software collects real-time equipment performance data. We also host small group seminars, focusing on specific products or aspects of our system. Our users love the opportunity to participate in this interactive experience, and we have witnessed numerous sales occur as a direct result of a customer's visit to a display center.

In addition to generating interest in our systems and more easily allowing us to respond to customer questions, the display centers have also served as an incredible resource for training our sales and service teams (resulting in better service and more satisfied users). They provide additional R&D "labs" outside of our facility in Pennsylvania.

Every time we come up with a major new idea, we wonder why we didn't think of it years earlier. I think there is a lesson here: we need to think harder and be more open-minded. It is also true that companies evolve, and in the case of display centers, it would have been difficult to meet this challenge and execute it a decade earlier.

A MILESTONE IN SALES

Today, CaptiveAire has one hundred sales offices and over 220 sales personnel covering most of North America. We continue to add about five sales offices per year to gain market share and provide for specialized markets. We have some overlapping distribution, so a major challenge we face is keeping our sales teams competing on a fair and friendly basis. This can be difficult at times because salespeople are aggressive and competitive, but by and large the system works extraordinarily well.

Our twenty-five year sales growth has averaged at thirteen percent each year in spite of some set backs and recessions. My focus is on making solid long-term decisions in consultation with our team. There are times when the sales team does not agree, but if I am sure of the decision, I push forward. If I am wrong, I acknowledge the error, take full responsibility, and change course.

Our sales force is highly stable, with very little turnover. We have worked hard to gain cooperation between our sales teams and our finance, engineering, marketing, IT, human resources, manufacturing, and service departments. Today we have a smoothly running, highly productive sales and marketing system that has produced steadily increasing growth for the past thirty years.

KEY TAKEAWAYS:

- Personally manage all sales efforts, as growth depends directly on the effectiveness of your sales team.

- Recognize that the User is King. Maintain a fanatical focus on the customer.

- Find every possible way to exceed your customer's expectations every time. Remember that you can't substitute style for substance.

- Hire the right people up front, and place them in the role best suited for them. If you help each employee fulfill his or her potential, everyone wins.

- Provide extensive training as needed to ensure all employees execute at a level of excellence.

- Always be open-minded to new ideas. You never know what great idea might change the future of your company.

"A teacher affects eternity.
He can never tell where his influence stops."

HENRY B. ADAMS

EDUCATION

Entrepreneurs are often highly energetic, and have trouble sitting still in the classroom. They are driven by their own curiosities, ambitions, and desires, and are frequently hands-on learners, not particularly suited to classroom learning. In some respects they are poorer for this. But in other respects, those entrepreneurs who daydream through school or skip it altogether are freed from conventional thinking, conventional wisdom, and conventional limits.

Michael Dell, Founder and CEO of Dell, Inc., is a good example. He attended the University of Texas, but didn't finish. In his freshman year he started an informal business selling upgrade kits for PCs. By age twenty-seven he became the youngest CEO to have his company achieve a ranking in *Fortune Magazine's* top 500 corporations. Of course, to today's readers, this is no surprise. The technology boom of the past fifty years has encouraged many young students to quit school, start a business, and become extraordinarily successful. Steve Jobs (Apple), Mark Zuckerberg (Facebook), Bill Gates (Microsoft), Richard Branson (Virgin Group), and Larry Ellison (Oracle) are but a few of the most well known.

As a student, I enjoyed learning but sometimes became impatient with the process. Formal education has much value if delivered properly: it provides the basic information, the combined knowledge from thousands of years of human experimentation and thought, as well as the intellectual development we require. But as an adult it frustrates me that too often, education is viewed as a sequence of courses leading to a degree and the end of our education, rather than the beginning of the lifelong learning process. Students receive a degree and become a doctor, accountant, nurse, engineer, teacher, or some other occupation, and believe their education is complete.

Although we should focus on mastering every course we take in school, in order to form a solid foundation of basic knowledge, we must also learn how to learn. Simply earning a degree is not sufficient because the world of knowledge is constantly changing; a student must develop the skills for thinking critically and utilizing the abilities of the human mind. While in college, I took the blended learning approach—I went to class and learned all I could, expanding my knowledge base and learning how to learn, and then began experimenting in entrepreneurial pursuits at night. This afforded me the best of both worlds—developing the mind while also gaining real skills and experiences that would enable me to build CaptiveAire from the ground up some years later.

BROAD-BASED EDUCATION

It is helpful to learn disciplines that differ from those with which we are familiar. For example, I majored in finance but realized it would be helpful to become technically competent as well to keep up with the ever-changing technological advances in our society. As time has passed, I have realized that developing these skills was indeed extremely beneficial, as the modern world is defined by the use of multiple technologies in virtually every aspect of business and everyday life. Unfortunately, some people do not take advantage of these critical opportunities to increase their knowledge and they are determined to remain ignorant about other subjects. You often hear them declare, "I don't do math" or other such statements. This mindset is not a luxury afforded by successful entrepreneurs.

Instead of narrowing your studies to a concentration in one subject, I would like to challenge you to expand your horizons. A broad-based education with a wide range of experience and knowledge is necessary for entrepreneurs in the dynamic world of growth, competition, and change.

Industries are constantly evolving, and most individuals in the 21st century find themselves working in a variety of arenas over time. My father taught my siblings and me from a young age to explore many disciplines. He often reasoned that if you can learn one discipline, you have the capacity to also master many others. Einstein similarly spoke of how much his understanding of mathematics was enhanced by his music education.

QUESTIONING AUTHORITY

Despite the merits of formal education, we should keep in mind that some of the things we learn in the classroom can be wrong, improved upon, or perhaps we failed to learn them correctly to begin with. In addition, educational institutions often lag behind the most advanced ideas and concepts in industry, because they are slow to change accepted notions and often refer back to outdated sources.

The key to making the most of your education is determining which ideas, methods, and concepts can and should be changed. However, an understanding of the classic principles of science and the humanities are important for our success, as it would not be useful to redefine the laws of gravity, for example.

Thinking skills are critical to the advancement of knowledge and ideas. In this age of the explosion of information, our ability to discriminate is even more crucial, especially with social media and Wikipedia-like publications.

Entrepreneurs are dreamers and have a disdain for process and conventional wisdom. We should use this momentum to innovate and make connections to form new and better ideas, but it is imperative that we learn deliberative, logical methods and carefully think through each move. It is also helpful to review our thinking again in a day or so as our subconscious mind processes information over time, ensuring that we are better prepared to make an informed decision.

CONTINUOUS LEARNING

The dynamics of the fast-paced business world require people who are lifelong, intrinsically motivated learners and thinkers. Decisions must be made quickly, which requires a well thought out, strategic philosophy of business and a broad knowledge base. I am a voracious reader of books (roughly twenty-five per year), periodicals, and management information, and I encourage all entrepreneurs to be the same. These learning endeavors improve our thinking processes and lead to more efficient problem solving. Entrepreneurs must be curious about everything relevant to their businesses.

Modern information technology allows us to constantly review and learn. What we don't know, we Google. Entrepreneurs utilize theory to achieve practical outcomes for users. We search for new products, technologies, and components, and sometimes when we don't find them we must invent our own. Our formal education prepares us for life, but continuous learning improves our knowledge and skills throughout life.

Work and practical experiences at an early age are also a critical part of our education because we begin to learn how to function in the workplace. Many of the famous entrepreneurial stories include the mention of a wide variety of jobs during the formative years. Early jobs can help us in our academic life because we know that there is a practical application to the subjects we are studying. Employers want students with diverse experiences and a demonstrated ability to learn and grow in a dynamic environment. Real work experiences are best for this type of learning, rather than simulated responsibility in university clubs and extracurriculars. While those involvements can be beneficial, most employers would much prefer the candidate who has proven himself in the real world.

EDUCATING OTHERS

One of the greatest challenges for an entrepreneur or business owner is recruiting. It is enormously difficult to find candidates with the appropriate sets of skills. Over the years, too many of CaptiveAire's employees have been inadequately prepared for the workplace; in my opinion due to failures of the existing public school system. We develop employees in many areas, but they must possess good values, a solid work ethic, and a love of learning, traits which can usually only be grasped during an individual's early education.

Over time, I have realized that the most important need for economic growth and society is the improvement of education, including character and skills development. Well-developed individuals are necessary for a productive society, and children must have a structured and thorough education in order to grow into virtuous and contributive members of our communities. Unfortunately, the vast majority of educational institutions in America are not serving our students adequately. Students in the U.S. are repeatedly falling behind their peers in other developed nations.

Entrepreneurs continually operate as problem solvers, so naturally I decided to begin to tackle this educational problem head on some years ago. In 1997, I decided to run for the Wake County school board in Raleigh. I won the first round, but lost in the final election. I was initially disappointed, but in retrospect, this turned out to be a positive for me. Like most entrepreneurs, I am frustrated by the amount of bureaucracy in the public sector, the slow speed at which most public agencies operate, and the degree to which they cling to the old rather than embrace the new.

I soon began thinking about my goals and decided that there might be another, and possibly better, way to achieve them. Determined entrepreneurs usually have full confidence that if their first plan doesn't work, there are multiple avenues for effecting change.

The previous year I had been a consultant on a charter school bill that was eventually passed by the North Carolina General Assembly, allowing for one hundred public charter schools to open in the years to come. Charter schools are funded by the state but are run by private boards under a charter or contract with the state. They represent an opportunity to redefine how schools are operated and allow operators to bypass many faddish norms.

FRANKLIN ACADEMY

While running for the school board, I began the process of opening a public charter school in Wake Forest, North Carolina. I did not realize it at the time, but I was on my way to becoming an educational entrepreneur.

In October of 1997, I gathered a team and together we opened a K-12 charter school that I named "Franklin Academy" (named after Ben Franklin, a man I greatly admire). The school, which opened in 1998, is now one of the largest public charter schools in the state, and has an annual waiting list of over 1,800. Over the next twenty years, Franklin Academy, named a "School of Excellence" by the State of North Carolina, will graduate over 2,500 students who are thinkers with strong academic and leadership skills. We believe these students will profoundly impact our community and state.

Franklin Academy represented a good start, but unfortunately North Carolina did not allow charter schools to expand beyond the first one hundred charters at that time. A few years after its founding, I began to review other school options and venues to continue growing my mission.

SAINT THOMAS MORE ACADEMY

In the year 2001, I was approached by several local families about establishing an independent Catholic high school. I had attended sixteen years of Catholic school myself and I appreciated my faith-filled education. Independent Catholic schools are a relatively new concept—Catholic bishops now allow schools to be operated by private individuals based on a contractual agreement and specified performance. After gathering a board of local Catholic leaders, we created Saint Thomas More Academy to offer a classical curriculum to high school students. STMA students build a rigorous foundation in Latin, logic, philosophy, and the sciences.

St. Thomas More Academy students are consistently accepted into top-notch universities, and the school has been recognized as one of the "Top 50 Catholic High Schools in America." We emphasize academics and character formation, infused with the tenets and traditions of Roman Catholicism.

Our graduates have grown into great thinkers and scholars. In fact, one of them, Holly Wiggin, works for CaptiveAire and contributed to the research and editing process for this book. Others have interned at CaptiveAire, assisted in political efforts, attended law and health professional schools, and even returned to teach the next generation of our students at St. Thomas More Academy.

THALES ACADEMY

With a waiting list of nearly 1,800 students per year trying to gain admission to Franklin Academy, and a limited number of slots available each year due to the state cap on expansion, I soon began to ponder opening a chain of private, secular, college preparatory schools that addressed all grade levels. In 2007, we incubated a new school in a dedicated space in the back of our corporate office. Initially K-2, Thales Academy now provides a pre-kindergarten through 12th grade education, with six campuses in Raleigh and the surrounding areas and five additional campuses in development.

Our utmost goal at Thales is to develop our students to their fullest potential. Time and time again we have seen even the most challenged students gain confidence as they begin to acquire knowledge and skills. We apply a "whole student" approach, educating for success in all aspects of life and career. Our comprehensive formation begins with a solid foundation in grades Pre-K-5 through the use of Direct Instruction. The effectiveness of this instructional method has been demonstrated in numerous educational studies over the past half century. Our formation continues in the junior high and high school grades with a rigorous classical curriculum that develops critical reasoning skills. In all grades, character formation and technical and non-cognitive skills development are emphasized to ensure all students are fully prepared for life.

Thales Academy is a highly innovative school and thus implements creative programs to assist in learning opportunities. We have implemented the Luddy Institute of Technology, a dual-track option to Thales students in grades 8-12 who are interested in a technologically geared career. Students have the opportunity to take pre-engineering courses, prepare for engineering studies, and engage in paid internships and apprenticeships. This track provides excellent career preparation, and teaches important skills such as developing competence in technological applications and financial management.

Currently, Thales Academy has six campuses operating and five additional locations under development. Thales is the largest private Pre-K-12 school group in North Carolina. My goal is to expand to at least twenty-five schools in the coming years, although I could easily envision many more. We hope to positively impact thousands of families across the U.S. and inspire others to improve education in their communities.

OUTCOME-BASED EDUCATION

At CaptiveAire, we focus on outcomes in all of our endeavors, and we do the same with all of our schools. Students are well prepared academically as scholars with well-developed thinking and communication skills and a thirst for continuous learning. In addition, the instruction we use to develop character ensures that our students graduate not only as cooperative and contributing members of society, but also as moral ones, well equipped to discern truth and make good decisions. From the start, we focus on imbuing them with a strong personal and work ethic and with the ability to regulate their emotions and show concern for others.

We believe this combination creates effective and ethical leaders who display the good judgment, critical thinking, and problem solving abilities necessary for employment in the 21st century. We research and employ numerous strategies and methods for ensuring that every student who passes through our doors is well formed and fully developed so that he or she can become a successful and virtuous member of our community.

We employ only teachers who are passionate about teaching and mentoring, are experts in their subjects, and are committed to delivering the best possible outcomes every day. We use yearly performance reviews and no tenure to keep standards high. Ultimately, we hold each teacher responsible for a great outcome, but parents, teachers, and students are all closely connected and support each other in the pursuit of excellence in learning.

Over time, these entrepreneurial schools have helped change the educational debate in North Carolina. Many people now realize that traditional public school education is not the only way. Developing a spirited team with a "can do" attitude greatly impacts the world. This is what we want our students to become—devoted family members and individuals who are eager to make a difference.

In addition to providing a strong education to future generations, it is important to ensure that all children have access to these opportunities. Every child must have a fighting chance to fulfill his or her potential and pursue personal aspirations. Our private schools charge the lowest tuition possible to ensure that all students have access to an excellent education. We maintain a strict budget, cutting costs whenever possible without harming quality. We do not fundraise, because I find it extremely annoying and we desire to teach our students to be self-reliant rather than search for handouts. We do accept donations for a tuition scholarship fund, but we do not solicit support and funds are used strictly for tuition scholarships only. Every effort is needed to produce educational options that are available to all children, regardless of socioeconomic background or previous family history.

These educational endeavors have provided enormous satisfaction and a sense of mission for me and for all of my associates who have helped create these schools over the past twenty years. I am pleased and thankful to have had the opportunity to develop and embolden some of our nation's future leaders.

THE TOP 15 OUTCOMES

In all of the Luddy Schools, we teach the Top 15 Outcomes, which are the fifteen traits and skills we hope each student will have mastered by the time they complete our programs and graduate. These Outcomes were developed after noticing the areas in which many individuals fail due to a flawed educational system. They also represent the necessary skills crucial for fulfilling one's highest potential. We believe that by studying the Outcomes daily for many years, our students will be far better prepared to succeed and contribute to the world.

1. **UNFAILING INTEGRITY** compels a person to follow a strong code of ethics with honesty in all situations.

2. **A COOPERATIVE AND CONTRIBUTIVE TEAM MEMBER** knows how to collaborate to achieve successful results.

3. **A VIRTUOUS LEADER WITH WELL-DEVELOPED JUDGMENT** combines thinking skills and traits such as humility, generosity, and courage.

4. **A STRONG WORK ETHIC** links perseverance, reliability, and honesty.

5. **SELF-RELIANCE** creates confidence to depend on one's own powers and resources to meet all of one's needs.

6. **DREAMS AND ASPIRATIONS TO CHANGE THE WORLD** help us remember that directed efforts bring us closer to our goals.

7. **A TRUTH SEEKER** searches for the correct, right, or accurate explanation of reality, following the scientific method.

8. **TRADITIONAL AMERICAN VALUES AND ENTREPRENEURIALISM** drive a leader to build and sustain a thriving economy.

9. **A CRITICAL THINKER** discerns the truth of a statement or observation through questioning and examination.

10. **WELL-DEVELOPED PEOPLE & COMMUNICATION SKILLS** promote effective sharing with a clear message.

11. **A CONTINUOUS LEARNER** takes lessons from all aspects of life and work, learns from mistakes, and adapts to change.

12. **GRATITUDE** acknowledges the gifts one has been given and the contributions of others.

13. **COMPETENT TECHNICAL SKILLS** allow individuals to join modern technological industries and navigate modern life.

14. **A HEALTHY MIND, BODY, AND SPIRIT** offer the freedom to operate at an optimal level and achieve a higher sense of fulfillment.

15. **ASTUTE PROBLEM SOLVING** leads one to identify the solutions to a problem, evaluate likely outcomes, assess risk, and choose correctly.

UNIVERSAL PRINCIPLES

Over the past twenty years, the Luddy Schools have been extraordinarily successful, with over 4,000 students currently enrolled throughout the Raleigh area. I strongly believe that this success is due to the lessons we've learned through the management of CaptiveAire.

The concepts in this book can be applied to virtually any endeavor, whether it be ventilation, education, or any other venture. The keys to CaptiveAire's success are the same as the keys to our schools' success: high quality, affordable products and service; relentless focus on the customer; careful financial management; rejection of the status quo; pursuit of excellence in all aspects; daily continuous improvement; outcomes orientation; integrity in all we do; decentralized management; robust quality control; and the list goes on.

The Luddy Schools have the advantage of forty-plus years of entrepreneurial management behind them, and they are just another example proving that these methods work.

KEY TAKEAWAYS:

- Use formal education to build a solid foundation of knowledge and learn how to learn. Use informal education to continuously improve your knowledge and skills.

- Study a broad range of disciplines. You never know when connecting the dots of multiple subjects may prove useful.

- Use logic and critical reasoning to think through all knowledge and determine the truth. There are many falsehoods and half-truths available; your job is to uncover the truth.

- Learn continuously. Most millionaires read an average of at least one book per month.

- Share your knowledge with others; we all win through shared success.

"Everyone has his own specific vocation or mission in life; everyone must carry out a concrete assignment that demands fulfillment. Therein he cannot be replaced, nor can his life be repeated. Thus, everyone's task is unique as is his specific opportunity to implement it. "

VIKTOR E. FRANKL

AFTERWORD

Forty years ago, I could not have imagined that CaptiveAire would be what it is today. Those years have yielded many valuable lessons and insights, which I have tried to impart in these chapters. Most big dreamers encounter many naysayers along the way, and I have had my share; fortunately I did not let them deter me.

A major key to CaptiveAire's success has been the ability to stay focused on the basics, no matter how large or complex we grow. Since that first day of business in November 1976, we've continually oriented everything we do around the needs of our customers. We ensure that every process, every new product or operation, brings value to the user.

Today, we have a growing team of 1,200 employees spread throughout the U.S. It is easy to overcomplicate things and become complacent at this size. Daily, we remind ourselves to remain humble, fight the temptations to think like a large company, and continually improve our performance and efficiency. Sometimes that requires fighting or removing the blockers within our own walls; it's a painful but imperative process.

The principles outlined in this book are the keys and the daily modus operandi of our organization. For forty years, we've worked hard to find and implement the best theories of management, economics, science, and engineering. This process requires a continuous flow of new ideas, a high level of alertness and critical thinking, curiosity, and the perseverance to test and experiment ideas continuously to find the best solutions. Individuals have to appreciate change to work at CaptiveAire. Everything is constantly in flux due to continuous improvement, and nothing is certain. For the average worker, this can be perplexing, because most people balk at the unfamiliar. For the entrepreneur, change is all we know. Most everything in the entrepreneurial world is unknown. Our job is to be comfortable being uncomfortable.

Humility is mandatory for best results. Dr. Peterson often stated, "None of us gets it all right." We must question ourselves and each other daily, and gratefully accept others' ideas and criticism. This is easy if we consider our mutual purpose and end goal to be top priority. As humans, we're all moving toward failure, but with a culture of humble cooperation, we help each other overcome our own deficiencies. Our top leaders frequently disagree with each other and with me, but all are open to hearing the other's point. If we're all working to provide long-term value to the user, the disagreements and failed ideas aren't an issue. We don't allow personal biases to get in the way. We just work together to find the best solutions.

I have always believed in the American Dream. In our country, you can accomplish anything you desire, as long as you are willing to pay your dues. I refuse to believe those who say the world is getting worse. My optimism, learned from my mother, has served me well. I feel extraordinarily blessed to live in this land of freedom and opportunity, and I encourage you to take full advantage of it, in whatever you pursue.

As a young man starting out, I recognized that my skill deficiencies and lack of business knowledge were impediments to running a large company. This led me on a lifetime's search for answers, solutions that helped me to grow incrementally. I quickly learned that you don't have to know all the answers up front; you just have to be willing to find them using every possible resource. I hope this book has proven to be a valuable guide for you in your own search for answers. I wish you the best as you embark on your own life's journey.

ABOUT
THE AUTHOR

Robert L. Luddy is the Founder and President of CaptiveAire Systems, Inc., a large privately held manufacturing company based in Raleigh, NC. He was born on July 9, 1945, in Miami, FL, and grew up in Harrisburg, PA. Luddy graduated from LaSalle University in Philadelphia, PA, in 1967 with a bachelor's degree in Finance. He served in the U.S. Army in Vietnam.

Luddy has a passion for entrepreneurship. He was awarded the 2007 Ludwig von Mises Entrepreneurship Award for "entrepreneurial success and devotion to the free-market ideal." He currently serves on many boards including the Calvin Coolidge Presidential Foundation and the Mises Institute. He regularly speaks about entrepreneurial development and leadership, regulations affecting business, and education in a variety of media (both locally and at the national level).

He has founded several schools, including Franklin Academy (a public charter K-12 school), St. Thomas More Academy (an independently owned Catholic high school), and Thales Academy (a growing chain of independent Pre-K-12 classical schools). Together his schools enroll nearly 5,000 students.

Luddy lives in Raleigh, NC, with his wife, Maria. He has two adult children and four grandchildren.